Creating harmonious relationships...

I0789354

Arthur Hill & Oswald Howard

ISBN: 9798662687776

PREFACE

Is it possible to create an ideal relationship?

Alas, our world is structured in such a way that there is no ideal relationship, never has been and never will be - this is a bitter reality. And do not rush to draw conclusions if it seems to you that some close friend, acquaintance, or even relative with the spouse has an ideal relationship.

Very often in public, the couple does not advertise personal troubles and problems, showing only the ideal side of the relationship (they have everything perfectly, they understand each other perfectly), but at home, behind closed doors, a scandal immediately begins ("You didn't do that, you didn't say! And indeed - why did we go there ?! ").

In rare cases, there are situations when partners are really happy with each other, but as a rule, this is the result of several years of work (or even tens of years!) On themselves and their relationships.

All people are different - someone likes historical facts, someone architecture, ancient artifacts or curious facts. However, it doesn't matter at all if the topic of dialogue becomes interesting to one of the partners, first of all, there should be an interest in a loved one - what affected him and why?

In any relationship, the contact itself is important, which is established directly in the dialogue, when partners communicate on the topic of each other's interests.

Contents

- Relationship Components
- The most important reason for problems in relations
- Passive aggression in relationships

- Ideal relationships
- Signs of an unhealthy relationship
- End of relationship
- The secret to harmonious relationships
- What is the difference between love, affection and dependence ?
- Where jealousy comes from
- Codependency and counter-dependence
- Irritation, anger, anger and rage
- The mechanism for the development of love addiction
- Myths about true love
- How to understand that this is your man
- Whether to leave the partner
- What to do if the husband is often angry
- Why the choice of loneliness will not bring you happiness
- Does the partner compete with you?
- The partner is often offended
- They don't hear me ...
- The partner blames you all the time
- Your partner is a psychopath
- Why a man loses interest in a woman
- Why do good girls fall for bad boys
- Fear of being abandoned
- Passion in relationships
- Get out of a toxic relationship
- Poisoning humor in relationships
- Difficulties of remarriage
- Family scenarios in relationships

Relationship Components

Relationships in a pair include three levels of interaction.

To make it clearer, pay attention to your body and conditionally divide it into three levels:

the level of sexual relations (I think you understand where this level originates conditionally),

the spiritual, emotional level (conditionally the solar plexus region)

the intellectual level (where I think everyone clear too).

All three levels of interaction manifest themselves in one way or another in family relationships and it is good when each of these levels finds its satisfaction in a pair. The fullness of these same levels and satisfaction in each individual level constitute a common, conditionally, call the relationship bank.

The fullness of this bank determines the quality of your relationship with a partner, the more full the relationship bank is, the more likely the relationship will be in times of crisis that cannot be avoided in family life.

I'll start from the bottom level- sexual level. The significance of this level is very exaggerated at the initial stages of the relationship, but at the same time depreciates already in deep family relationships. Sex is one of the basic needs of a person at the level of food. Sex, for our primitive brain, is a way to survive, to continue ourselves in the offspring, and, just as from food, nature was conceived to receive special satisfaction from this process. Satisfaction with sexual life is a kind of indicator of relationships and its foundation, when there is sex in a married couple, there is a relationship, when it is not, it is an indication that something is wrong or will be wrong if sex does not appear soon it is worth making a reservation that it is an indicator of the norm in sex; everything is individual here and depends on your joint appetites. Of course, the sexual level is the foundation, but not the foundation of the relationship.

The presence of the following levels is important for a successful life together. The emotional or emotional level is the level of your emotional closeness, sympathy. This level very much embraces us in a state of falling in love at the beginning of a relationship and often leaves a veil in the eyes of lovers. The emotional intensity of this level decreases over time and, as a rule, opens up many new unexpected features of our partner, and usually a man becomes sober from this inebriated intoxication faster.

The level of mind is the level at which, ideally, it is recommended to start a family relationship, when drunkenness from love falls off.

This is the level of common sense of whether a partner is suitable for you in your outlook on life, life principles and guidelines. There are cultures where marriage is concluded by mutual agreement of the parents or after a special established custom, for example, engagement. Here, specific rules are stipulated that the family will follow and this position is not without meaning.

It is believed that if partners are ideally suited to the level of understanding of life together and the distribution of obligations, then the level of feelings then comes as a result of awareness of the perfect fit to each other. The importance of the level of mind can be imagined as a vessel, where the image of the vessel is the rules and norms that will be observed in the family or family traditions. But the contents of the vessel water - the image of the emotional, emotional component of the relationship.

Just as a cracked vessel cannot hold the flowing water, the difference in understanding the rules of family life and other things, the one who expects what from family relationships, destroys the most sincere and deep feelings of spouses.

Therefore, before starting a family, it is worth specifying your ideas about how you see family relationships, what is the role of women and men, who occupies a leading role in earning and providing for a family. Do not underestimate the importance of this item.

I'll give you a private life example: a girl who went on a date with a guy understood for granted that the same way a young man pays for joint walks will also be in family life: he will take all the financial support of the family on himself, while for the guy , which was raised by a single mom, it is secretly clear that a woman is able to earn and provide for her family herself and for him the norm at the level of the deep unconscious in family life is to give the right to provide a family to a woman or to share this right with her in half. And so they live afterwards with mutual claims and are perplexed about what is not clear. And the last relationship is the stronger, the more common binding threads in them.

For example: a stamp in a passport, a common surname, an apartment bought with joint money, conscientious children, etc. Having similar binding partners of the thread, a kind of bond occurs between them.

And in such cases it will not be so easy to slam the door and leave, at least it will be necessary to solve joint issues on the separation of the connecting threads, and while you will solve them, you will look and agree

The most important reason for problems in relations

What primarily spoils relations between partners, exacerbating an already oppressive situation?

Constant demands (on the female side) and constant expectations (on the part of men).

Waiting often happens in silence, sometimes even the person himself does not understand what exactly he is waiting for.

Against this background, dissatisfaction manifests itself all the time - and the partner seems to be the one, but something else needs to be "smoothed", combed (better work, clothing style needs to be changed, he should look after himself, he should pay more attention and give flowers more often, drive to the cinema, does not help at home and does not put toilet paper in the common basket, doesn't remove plates from the table, doesn't wash dishes, etc.).

As a rule, this entire list is constantly changing. For example, a partner began washing dishes and helping, but now does not expose a new toilet paper roll when it runs out. So, already exhibits, excellent, but here we are not going to the cinema now!

Over time, all these requirements and expectations grow, grow, grow. In conjunction with them, the problem begins to aggravate the lack of gratitude to each other for what each partner brings in a couple. If I learned how to immediately wash the dishes at the request of a loved one, it cost me some effort, and it's important for me to appreciate my actions ("What a fellow you are! So suddenly you suddenly became closer to my way of seeing life!"). It doesn't matter who performs what roles in the pair, you need to notice what the partner is doing for the sake of your relationship. The wife cooks breakfast in the morning, brings the children to school, takes the child out of the kindergarten, or the husband does it - say "thank you" from time to time for these seemingly daily chores.

For example, in the evening after a hard day's work ("I now thought that you would bring a child every day to a kindergarten or school in the morning. If I had to wake up 3 hours before work, I would not be enough for a long time. I am so grateful to you!") . We all have great difficulties with gratitude. It's hard for us to say "thank you" or ask another person about something ("Listen, could you ..."), instead the request turns into an instruction ("So you have to! This is your child, so let's take him to school! ").

If you translate the tone from the requirements to the request, from depreciation and indifference to gratitude, the relationship in the pair will change for the better. A person may refuse to comply with your instructions, may even run far away from you.

There is always a choice how to live, and if life with a partner is unbearable, and every day begins with thinking whether it is worth staying, but at the same time make incredible efforts to build relations brick by brick, one day your loved one can make a choice not for your favor. Be thankful!

At joint sessions of psychotherapy, partners are often given the following task: one should express gratitude to the other for everything that he does for him ("I see that you make breakfast every day, get up half an hour earlier. I really appreciate it and am grateful!") . As a rule, at the time of a pause, the second partner begins to say something in response: "Yes, but it's not so difficult!" However, it is very important to accept gratitude, to hear and to accept at your own expense all those kind words that speak to you. You make certain efforts and do not lie in bed at this moment. Through several interactions, relationships, even stalled, with aggression and irritation, become warmer. We just forget to notice and say nice and kind words to the partner. We do not have this habit - to ask and give thanks.

Develop this positive habit, try to change your mentality, develop new thinking and mentality. And here is an important point - for this you must always watch your life and listen to yourself.

The ability to thank life for what we have is a great skill to work with. We often complain about what we don't have, but it's wrong! Switch from such complaints to positive points ("Yes, I don't have the $ 1,000,000 I need now, but I have a family, a house, food! Thanks for that, and the money is earned!",

"I don't have a boyfriend, but I have a beautiful work and friends, the right skills, I learned a lot. "

Look always positive.
Undoubtedly, your needs will always grow, it's good and right, but don't forget the path traveled - thank yourself for this and the person who helped you in this.

Passive aggression in relationships

In a pair, one of the partners is hysterical, screaming, cursing, something does not suit him in a relationship, he expresses his displeasure, and the second one in such situations either sits silently and smiles, or says: "Are you probably a hysterical? You're insane! "Why is this happening?

Passive aggression is a person's behavior in which any external manifestations of anger are suppressed through implicit, casual pronounced insults, gloomy and displeased behavior, stubbornness, refusal to perform any other sediments, etc.

In the above example, passive aggression is characteristic of a partner who will sit and smile. This phenomenon is quite common, it is especially noticeable when couples come to a family consultation with a psychotherapist - a woman proves something, screams, all in tears, and outwardly her behavior can really be characterized by an insane state, but the partner is calm and claims that in this situation, it's not about her (or a man may "openly" be indignant: "Well, see, see, what's happening ?!").

The partner launches a woman's tantrum with his behavior. If people live together for more than 3-5 years (sometimes there are situations of 20 years too!), he probably knows what phrases can provoke such behavior. As a rule, the mechanism of projective identification works here, when a person himself denies all his feelings of anger, anxiety, guilt, which the other experiences in contact with him.

In practice, this is quite interesting. For example, you agreed to meet with a friend, but then you decided to change the venue ("Listen, I can't get there, let's meet here?"). So, you met and immediately asked: "Is everything all right, what is the meeting here?" A few minutes passed, the conversation started, and your friend suddenly makes you understand that because of you he had unmet needs ("Due to the fact that we met here and not where we originally agreed, I can't do what was planned ! "). To your remark about what you had to say about it right away, a person is trying to evade an open conflict ("Yes no, no, everything is in order!"). So what do we have?

First, "everything is in order", then a weak injection of aggression, which is even impossible to grasp because of tight boundaries (besides, a person cannot get to his feelings himself!) And defenses to protect the Ego, a firm conviction that he is good , white and fluffy hare. As a rule, if you read this article, you are on the side of that person who has hysteria and outbreaks of aggression.

If your partner has leaked his aggression, it is you who will think about what is happening. In fact, he defended himself, his feelings do not live out, and you all feel for him and you feel either stupid or guilty of whatever, or you are being eaten up by anxiety.

If all the time while a person is telling you something, you are experiencing excitement and anxiety, we are talking about repressed anxiety. How to get out of the "trap" in which you fall?

In fact, this is quite difficult. It is important not to get involved in a state of guilt, anxiety, fear, aggression, tension, etc. (if you can't resist these feelings and react sharply, then you have your own tension, fears, guilt, aggression, etc., and your partner, relatively speaking, it strengthens them and forces them to take over). As a rule, people with passive aggression cannot directly speak out because in childhood they were often severely punished and scolded for it, but living with these feelings is very difficult for them.

Both partners need to work in pairs - both the passive aggressor and the one who provokes scandals. Own guilt, fear and shame, for which the manipulator and the aggressor "catches you", it is very difficult to work on their own. You need the support and help of a professional psychologist, so you should take the "Aggression as a Resource" course (the leading psychotherapist will ask you additional questions, check your homework, and encourage you to become more aware of the situation).

If something changes inside your mind, then there will be changes in contact. Your partner will not be able to manipulate you so deftly and in time he may have to realize the whole depth of the situation.

Another important point - in this contact you process the voltage of your partner. How to stop doing this, but do not swear with a partner?

A scandal is not the only option for the manifestation of aggression; one can say no to a person's feelings and refuse to get involved in his game. Such an approach is also aggression, the defense of one's borders. Only when you start moving in this direction will the partner try to sort out his feelings. Sooner or later it will happen! Do you want to eliminate the voltage in a pair?

Do not join the partner's game and learn to understand your own feelings (What feelings were hurt? What made you show such aggression?).

Ideal relationships

Is it possible to create an ideal relationship?

Alas, our world is structured in such a way that there is no ideal relationship, never has been and never will be - this is a bitter reality. And do not rush to draw conclusions if it seems to you that some close friend, acquaintance, or even relative with the spouse has an ideal relationship.

Very often in public, the couple does not advertise personal troubles and problems, showing only the ideal side of the relationship (they have everything perfectly, they understand each other perfectly), but at home, behind closed doors, a scandal immediately begins ("You didn't do that, you didn't say! And indeed - why did we go there ?! ").

In rare cases, there are situations when partners are really happy with each other, but as a rule, this is the result of several years of work (or even tens of years!) On themselves and their relationships.

There may be such an option - the partners look quite happy for others, they have an ideal relationship, but behind a closed door they are completely indifferent to each other.

In any relationship, there is an unspoken rule - this is hard and daily work on yourself. Nobody will read your thoughts, it's just impossible to get along perfectly with a partner - work on relationships! For the first six months (a year, one and a half, sometimes two years), the relationship in a couple may look ideal - during this period people are prone to the process of merging, therefore they are ready to adapt to the needs and desires of each other, they completely ignore the difference in character, interests and etc. Relations in a pair at the initial stage can be compared with a demo version of what will happen in a few years.

Over time, when the "halo of ideality" fades, partners begin to notice the difference in each other, and then problems arise. The basic principles of an ideal relationship:

1. Healthy adequate self-esteem, self-confidence, the ability to love and respect yourself and other people.

2. Confidence in yourself and your partner. Confidence in intimacy is the ability to be with a partner in intimacy, trusting him at the same time, and not be afraid of intimacy itself.

If a person has a trauma of attachment, as a rule, there will be problems with trusting intimacy (he will feel discomfort, fear of absorption and control, fear of absorbing his partner or, in general, harming relationships).

If trust is formed in a couple, the partners will not be afraid of punishment from each other, reproaches and comments - the beloved person will understand me, he is not going to hurt me. Against the background of sincere affection and open friendly relations, the ability to be vulnerable is formed, without which the couple simply will not have honesty. However, it is important to distinguish between the ability to be vulnerable and not vulnerable.

In the words of the partner you need to hear not an attempt to stab you, to hurt you more, but an attempt to understand. You do not need to hear your own pain in the requirements of a loved one. Quite often in this place we get into our own injuries associated with a period of unconscious development (up to 7 years) and relationships with the mother's object (it can be a mother, father, grandmother, grandfather, or all at the same time).

A healthy attachment arouses trust among partners, while not interfering with developing (manifesting) and being an individual - everyone can set goals and not be afraid of betrayal and rejection by a loved one.

3. Willingness to change - it is important to change, but not to change yourself. What does it mean?

You can't blindly obey a partner if he requires you to radically change your life values and attitudes, because of this a strong conflict can arise.

For example, a partner does not see anything wrong with robbing a bank or indulging in drugs, forcing you to follow his example.

If a person, for the sake of relations, goes against his own values, this will ultimately become not only a reason for the separation of partners from each other, but also a detrimental effect on the personality itself. It is worth changing in everyday matters - for example, banal quarrels over an unopened tube of toothpaste, a dirty mug after drinking coffee, an unmade bed, etc. You can easily come to terms with such trifles and understand - these habits are formed from childhood, aged 10-12 years (the period when love is instilled, or, conversely, a negative attitude to cleaning). However, re-educating a person in such matters is quite difficult (sometimes even impossible), he himself must have a desire and motivation to change. How to put up with the unbearable habits of a partner?

To get started, ask yourself why exactly you quarreled. Is it a value or a trifle for you?

If the situation as a whole is important to you (for example, remove the mug), you need to understand yourself, understand what exactly its value is and explain it to your partner. Is cleanliness and comfort for you? Or maybe a simple observance of the rules and regulations that guided your family (therefore, it is common for you to do this)? Or do you feel uncomfortable if the room is not cleaned?

Try to divide the territory of the apartment into personal (yours and your partner) and general. Thus, you will maintain order and cleanliness at home, and let the partner do whatever he wants. For a common area, you can draw up a shift schedule for cleaning.

In the context of the problem, it is very important to articulate the rules of the family system and to distribute the roles of everyone (who and what does). At first it will be difficult to follow these guidelines, but the main thing is that the partners have a desire to conduct a common economy, in which case they will eventually learn to move in one direction.

4. Willingness to work on yourself. Relationships are a reflection of childhood injuries. If in childhood the maternal figure was cold and repulsive, in adulthood a person will feel cold in every act of a partner. Moreover, out of habit, he will respond in accordance with his feelings and, as a result, after a while the partner will really start to feel cold.

So, relationships are hard work on oneself. It is necessary to live through all the complex feelings associated with the rejection of the mother, again. For a more effective result, it is worth attending psychotherapy sessions.

If you are working on a problem yourself, it is important to accurately understand and realize what kind of partner's actions there is an acute reaction to, exactly how they are associated with childhood. All experienced feelings were directed to a completely different person, but now you have focused them on your partner - the psyche is trying to complete an unfinished story.

Relatively speaking, a person was hurt, but no one apologized. And it doesn't matter if you have been asked forgiveness dozens of times, you still want someone to be held accountable. People who have experienced childhood trauma are not able to hear a partner, they want to hear the cherished words of apology from the mother's figure or the person who hurt in the past.

Quite often in a relationship a situation arises when one of the partners through the prism of perception (mother, father, grandparents - all those who said about him: "You are stupid, underdeveloped!") Hears something of his own.

As a result, each of the participants in the dialogue remained unconvinced. It is such moments that should be worked out very carefully. The more injuries and projections will be worked out, the more you open up to your partner and you can be extremely honest and sincere with him, you will have a vulnerability.

This step is an important step to gain understanding between partners. A dirty mug will sooner or later lead to an outbreak of anger, because in childhood one of the partners was punished for this - and only open relationships in a couple allow you to understand the true reason for his behavior. This is not just an outburst of anger or shame, it is a violent mental reaction, an affect associated with severe trauma received in childhood - knowing the origins of the situation, partners can more easily relate to each other's actions.

5. The manifestation of love for each other (not only in words but also in actions). In a pair it is very important that the partners have the same values in life and orientations. This will allow us to build joint plans for the future. For example, if one of the partners has the material component in the first place, and the second meditates for eight hours every day, these two people will never understand each other.

There is a very informative and interesting book by Gary Chapman "Five languages of love. How to express love to your companion. " Words of encouragement, time, gifts, help and touch - thanks to these methods, you can express your love to a partner.

Love is a feeling that constantly requires confirmation. Each of us wants to feel every day: "Yes, I still love", "Yes, they are waiting for me and understanding", "I am important", "They respect me", etc. Do not skimp and let the partner fully feel what he wants, then everything will turn out in a relationship.

Signs of an unhealthy relationship

Do you have a healthy relationship with a partner?

In total, 12 criteria can be distinguished that help to understand this rather complex and confusing issue.

If you have 1-3 positive points, it is worth considering and working out weak zones of relationships;

3-6 positive points - start packing your bags; more than 6 positive points - run away from your partner without even packing! What are these signs?

Partner is competing with you. In a healthy relationship, each of the partners perceives the other positively, enjoys his successes and achievements. However, the reverse situation is not uncommon - in relationships there may be undisguised envy and rivalry towards each other ("But I've done much better! Have you achieved something in life?"), Manifested in a derogatory tone during communication.
We all sometimes envy, but outside a healthy relationship, this feeling takes on a toxic character and ruins everything positive in the bud - the partner feels that he simply does not have the right to develop, because in return he will not hear bestowal and joy from a loved one.

- You feel depressed and depressed.
- You began to lose weight dramatically or, conversely, get better.
- You often fall into a state of apathy and depression, this prevents you from living normally, everything else becomes simply uninteresting.

All these signs can be evidence that there is an energy vampire next to you (for example, a narcissus or a psychopath), which sucks out your internal energy, immobilizes, takes all the accumulated resources (while it will be comfortable and convenient for him to be near you) .

You are always to blame for everything. In an unhealthy relationship, the partner is completely not ready to take responsibility, look at the world realistically - he "hides" his guilt all the time.

In a healthy relationship, everything happens the other way around - the partner is always ready to take part of the responsibility on himself, ready to talk about it honestly, directly and openly ("Good. Perhaps I said wrong here, I offended you in my own words, hurt you. Understand, please, you can't take my words so seriously! "). Relatively speaking, responsibility is divided equally.

Thus, if you understand that the partner is ready to listen and hear all that has been said, he assumes a share of his responsibility. For a healthy relationship, this is of no small importance.

However, quite often there are people who think that everything around is to blame, therefore, the partner will also be guilty (of who the president of the country is; in bad weather conditions; problems with friends, etc.).

Such individuals will always complain: "Again, this rainy weather! When will everything be all right? " As a result, psychological tension arises in the couple, which negatively affects the relationship as a whole.

The partner is trying to change you all the time. In mature and established relationships, people have already accepted each other for what they are. If the couple has problems with mutual understanding, then your partner will always find something to complain about (appearance, tone of voice, words, interests, hobbies, etc.). He will compare you with everyone, exclude from your life all the pleasant moments and situations that bring you pleasure.

The partner speaks only about himself. This is manifested in a cut-off at a glance ("How are you?" - "Good! Today was at work ..." - "Listen, but I have so much fun!").

At this moment, a person has a feeling that during a revelation, when he begins to excitedly share news, the partner is simply unbearable to listen to him. Why? Only he must appear in the conversation!

The partner often criticizes. You don't do it that way, don't start! Constant monitoring by the partner Frequent calls, meticulous questions (where are you, with whom are you, what are you wearing, who are you talking to).

A partner is trying to take control of your whole life, to completely manage it. From the outside, such behavior may seem like a concern, but in fact it is over-concern, sadism. Unreasonable and painful jealousy of a partner for everyone around him, accompanied by loud scandals, tantrums, checks of phone calls and messages, up to personal things.

If you begin to express your dissatisfaction about this behavior of the partner, he will continue to do so secretly. Relationships will increase in tension, your self-esteem will drop, your fear of your partner's anger will appear, in the end you will close at one point, stop talking with strangers, limit your social circle - "God forbid that your loved one is upset, and even more angry ! "

Frequent resentment partner. Almost any of your thoughtless words or actions causes tears, and an attempt to speak frankly leads to even greater resentment, claims against you begin. This maelstrom of resentment never ends - you are always guilty of everything! As a result, you really start to feel like a cruel and heartless monster towards this poor fellow.

The partner never learned your language of love, didn't understand what you like, what makes the heart beat faster. Until now, it's only important for him that he loves. You and your partner have different biorhythms, for the whole time of the relationship you did not get used to each other (you go to bed at ten in the evening, and the partner at four in the morning and, accordingly, wakes up in 12-15 hours of the day - as a result, you simply do not intersect with the person). In addition, there are situations that on your only day off he can play some game all night, watch TV, do some work or chat with friends online, and relax during the day.

You stopped having sex - the item is pretty commonplace, but important. This is an indicator that something does not suit the relationship of one of the partners, and the second silently agrees to this.

End of relationship

Why does a situation arise when the relationship "holds" you, although you understand very well that this is the end?

The most obvious and understandable reason for all prudent people is children. When the children are small, it is always a pity to leave them and deprive the father or mother.

In general, the situation of the collapse of the family is especially traumatic for people who did not have a mother or father, respectively, they remain in the most destructive relationships (if only the children were well!). What to do in this case?

To begin with, deal with the trauma associated with the father / mother, and then make a decision in relation to the children. If there is a very destructive relationship between parents (constant scandals and abuse), children are better off not seeing this, so you should not try to save the family in this situation.

There may be a different situation - mom and dad live their whole lives without love, tenderness and any kind of emotional contact, and if they swear, then all this happens quietly. In fact, people exist side by side. As a rule, in such a family, in adulthood, children copy the behavior of their parents, acting out the scenario seen earlier - they find a couple and simply "live" with a person without love and tenderness. At the same time, they suffer very much, but do not understand how to get out. You can find a way out, but it requires considerable time and effort - at least a year of therapy to understand all the nuances of childhood injury.

So, if you maintain a destructive relationship for the sake of children - this is all a lie and a provocation! All this is done exclusively for their own purposes, for their own sake! Fear of ending a relationship. Perhaps you have never lived on your own, and have not been separated from the parent figure.

If you didn't merge with the parental figure (in the normal sense), in this case separation is not possible, as well as separation from the husband / wife - in the human psyche there is no ability to distance oneself from the person, live independently and develop your life alone.

In general, many people are quite scared to live independently (relatively speaking, to go out into the big world alone), plan their life, achieve goals, etc. without help. You do not have confidence in your feelings. On a subconscious level, you understand that something is going wrong, you guess, you feel, but you don't listen to the sensations.

A good example from practice is the story of one of the clients, who all the time seemed that her husband was cheating on her. - It seems to me that the partner is cheating on me! - Okay, next? - Of course, I did not catch him for treason, he denies everything, but for so long I have not received flowers as a gift, I have not heard pleasant words. And indeed, our relationship is completely different from what it was before. - And before you had everything - and flowers, and emotional contact? "Before, yes." We spent more time together, he treated me gently and carefully. Now there is no such thing! - Good. So why are you still in a relationship then? - How why?! I didn't catch a partner on treason! In this situation, cognitive dissonance is clearly felt. Why do you need to catch a person on treason if you are no longer satisfied with your attitude to yourself? And it doesn't matter if the partner changes or not. He simply stopped treating you, as before, stopped loving (in fact, your love for him has evaporated - how can you love an indifferent person?).

Accordingly, a person seeks out a reason (quite compelling - treason!) In order to leave the relationship, but why is it necessary? It's much easier to just leave your partner and not say everything that's boiling ("Listen,

I've made the final decision. I don't know what and how are you, but in our relations there is no warmth and concern ...").

The reason for this behavior is some co-dependence based on guilt. I myself can't take responsibility, so I need to blame you, the only way I can get away from you. As a rule, such people very often provoke a partner for treason. Resisting such a thing is quite difficult - the partner exerts influence so much with his distrust, bad attitude, indifference and constant attacks ("What do you have?"). Sometimes in this case I want to answer: "Here you are! You were waiting, catch it! "

So, why do you stay in a relationship that has long become obsolete? You do not want to take responsibility, do not want to be an adult partner.

It is important to understand here - if you think your partner is an infantile person with a split mentality (which is why he cheats), who is afraid to take responsibility for anything, these are your projections. All this can be said directly about you. Nobody wants to hear such words, it is easier to establish oneself in one's own suspicion (the partner is an idiot, a bad person, infantile, etc.), and you are white and fluffy.

However, if you remain in a relationship with this person, reconcile with the fact that you are the same (perhaps you have it manifests itself in a slightly different degree, but still exists).

Any relationship has a specific purpose - for both partners and each separately. Quite often there is a situation where the relationship has completed its tasks and has become obsolete. Spouses talk about how they loved each other, everything was fine with them until they bought a car, house, apartment, raised and put their children on their feet. And suddenly, the husband and wife understand that the relationship has reached its goal, the joint project is over, and you can move on to the next relationship and other goals. The society has long moved away from the idea of when you can live with one partner all your life from and to, such couples are now rare.

Sometimes there are partners who have lived together for 15-20 years, have lived to be 80, but they constantly swear, are dissatisfied with something, etc. That is why, if people lived their whole lives together, this does not mean at all that their life was cloudless and happy.

Currently, there is a tendency towards consistent monogamy in the world - a person lives with one partner for several years, then with another, third, etc. In addition, each of the partners has personal goals in the relationship, and before you put an end to it, you need to figure out exactly what your goal was, what stage of the development of the psyche you pursued, being next to this person.

Relationships are always the growth of the soul, and if you have already felt its influence, this is a clear sign that the relationship has outlived itself. However, to make a final decision, do not rely solely on this statement, listen to yourself, look inside your consciousness - what did this person give you?

A common situation is that a woman enters into a relationship with a partner, like with a father (she needs a man like a father to console, help, take on most of the responsibility, etc.). Over time, she "grows up," and she no longer needs a father! At the same time, the partner continues to play the role of the pope, his task has not yet been closed (there may be a different situation - the task has been completed, but the person is scared to take a different position). Accordingly, in the pair there is an internal dissonance, people have already outlived themselves. If you feel that the relationship is over, but you can't say goodbye to a partner, figure out what exactly holds you, why you are in a state of co-dependence, feel guilty, and you are burdened with fear of taking responsibility.

Children are not the answer to such a question! The main thing for children is to see their parents happy. It is important how you explain to them everything, and how to present this important information. Be sure to communicate, because no matter that mom and dad broke up as a couple, they loved each other before and continue to love their child. It is important for any person at any age to understand that he is the fruit of the love of his parents, and what is happening now is life. And you don't need to hide your child for 18 years under a thick shell! He must see life as it is, otherwise - having entered the big world, a person will constantly fill up sore bumps.

Let it be better to hurt first, and then a little bit. Life is life, it is a cruel reality, a "bare truth." Another good reason to break off a relationship that has become obsolete is that you and your man deserve to love and be loved.

But even in this case, before making a final decision, figure out what function the relationship performed for you personally, what kind of person you entered into, what needs you met, and what needs to be worked out.

At this stage, you need to understand that you are in a relationship not because of codependency and fear of leaving them - there is something much more important. If there is nothing like this, you should not torture yourself and your soul mate, try to "glue something together."

Loneliness together - this is the most painful thing in the world!

The secret to harmonious relationships

Why do some couples live together their whole lives, while others separate after a few years?

The famous American psychotherapist and founder of The Gottman Institute, John Gottman, devoted his whole life to studying the issue of marital relations and developed a methodology for determining the prospects of marriage.

As a result of many years of research, the psychologist has established criteria by which it is possible to understand with accuracy up to 94% whether a couple will be together in 6 years. 130 couples were selected for research; each of them was monitored by a psychotherapist for one day. In the framework of the experiment, the conditions of the couple's joint life as close as possible to reality were created - living in one apartment and the freedom of action of each partner (someone reading a newspaper / book, watching TV, etc.).

During the day, while spending time together, each of the partners periodically tries to establish contact with the other, inviting them to participate in a dialogue ("Look, what a bird flew!", "Oh, look what the newspapers write", "But I thought you would say about this? "). The reaction of the partner in this case is of great importance. If he (she) is distracted, becoming interested in the interests of another (for example, pushes the newspaper away), and says "Where? Show me! Oh, how beautiful! ", This means that the partner accepted the invitation. If he (she) continues to do his own business, not paying attention to the comment, or dismisses ("Well, beautiful!"), This is a refusal of an invitation.

After analyzing the results, John Gottman concluded that couples with a high percentage of responses (87%) still lived together after 6 years, couples with a lower percentage of responses (33%) did not live together and 6 years or separated in the sixth year of marriage.

The key point is to become interested in the interests of the partner (regardless of your interests, it is absolutely not necessary that the topic raised interests you!).

If there is mutual understanding and love in a couple, each partner tries to make efforts to understand the other - why does a spouse wonder about some question, what is so surprising in the topic raised, why is this picture so beautiful?

All people are different - someone likes historical facts, someone architecture, ancient artifacts or curious facts. However, it doesn't matter at all if the topic of dialogue becomes interesting to one of the partners, first of all, there should be an interest in a loved one - what affected him and why?

In any relationship, the contact itself is important, which is established directly in the dialogue, when partners communicate on the topic of each other's interests. John Gottman identified two criteria necessary for a long-term relationship in a couple - magnanimity and kindness. It is thanks to these qualities that a person can put aside all his affairs and become interested in the partner's experiences and thoughts.

In fact, being able to put oneself and one's needs aside on time is a rather important aspect of successful relationships in a couple. This means that the partner has not only generosity, but also disinterested compliance and indulgence, allowing you to sacrifice your interests for the sake of a loved one. However, it is important to maintain balance.

If a person is kind and generous, over time he will meet the same partner. Why?

It is impossible to give and receive nothing in return all the time. There is a pattern - the more you give, the more they give you (provided that the relationship is not built with a narcissist or psychopath). Most people respond to generosity and kindness and want to give something in return.

That is why for a harmonious and balanced relationship it is important to first of all understand that the relationship is not the place where you just need to take it, you need to give it here.

If the partner gives with some expectation to get something in return, this indicates a lack of sincerity, honesty and complete emotional inclusion in the pair. Want a stable and lasting relationship?

In this case, it is worth revising your character of behavior in relation to the partner.

What is the difference between love, affection and dependence ?

The ability to love is a skill that is characteristic only for a highly developed psyche. If your psyche is deeply neurotic or at the level of a frontier organization, most likely you will demand a lot of attention to yourself, relationships will be important only for you, and not for your partner.

Individuals with a highly organized psyche are able to live for another person (in the context of the question, we are not talking about "completely dissolving in your partner", such relationships are neurotic) - think about his problems and take care. What is love?

This is an interest in the growth and development of your love object - you want your loved one to be happy, regardless of your interests, views and desires.

In the modern world it is impossible to be completely "giving", each of us wants to receive something in return. In this case, you need to be able to negotiate, find a compromise, make concessions, and here it is important to maintain at least some balance (it is not necessary to strive to achieve a 50/50 balance, a fairly comfortable balance directly for you).

For example, your partner is stubborn and not capable of giving in to anything, and you are loyal to concessions and always make contact - this situation is comfortable in a pair for both.

What is attachment?

Attachment - in fact, it is a children's need that exists in order for the child to survive. The kid is attached to his mother, walks behind her like a duckling, "tail" - for him it's safety, survival, ability to live, protection from any danger, etc. Relatively speaking, if a child stumbled and fell, but his mother is not there, this is for him a much greater danger than if it were nearby. This is the survival instinct - to be closer to mom. Outwardly, the situation looks like love, but in essence it is attachment at the level of instincts.

In the popular science book Dick Swaab, "We are our brain. From the uterus to Alzheimer, the process of forming attachment is very well described. First, the mother shows maternal behavior, takes care of the baby, worries about his safety, cherishes, cherishes, shows tenderness, turns on emotionally. In response to this, the child shows his affection for mom. Accordingly, if the mother's maternal instinct is weak, there is little attachment to the baby, he generally will not form the skill of attachment to people. Despite the fact that attachment is a childhood trait, in adulthood we become attached to each other.

Love and affection are very close and similar concepts, quite often follow in parallel to each other. It is impossible to love a person and not want to be near him, not to want him to hug, to devote some attention.

We live in a rather neurotic world, in a world of injuries and needs that cannot be eliminated, so it's important for us to feel affection, not to feel lonely, but at the same time we need to be attached to some extent to us.

Addiction is a very strong degree of attachment, painful when you cannot live without your partner. Conditionally - it's as if you had assigned some part of vital functions for your partner (for example, he prepares food, constantly accompanies you on trips to the theater or the cinema), and without him you don't feel like a full-fledged, integral person.

In fact, this is a thirst for possession, an unstoppable need for a partner's closeness, a desire to be with him as often and as long as possible (co-dependent relationship). All these feelings are accompanied by a painful sensation - if a partner leaves me, the world will simply collapse, a catastrophe will happen, and my life will be completely destroyed.

In general terms, dependence is a deep degree of attachment, overly painful, characteristic of those people who in childhood did not have a strong relationship with the mother's object (emotionally cold mother, not included in the life of the child). In such cases, a person will have a bias in adulthood - or he will fall into a codependent relationship, or into a counter-dependent.

Where jealousy comes from

Jealousy is one of the most powerful and pronounced emotions of a person. There is a whole stream of feelings in it - from despair, shame, resentment to anger, hatred, possibly even revenge. All these feelings accumulate in a person and prevent him from calmly thinking, breathing and living. What is jealousy?

Experts believe that this feeling is generated due to self-doubt, its value and constant fear of other people. Jealousy in a sense is isolation. A person who has been hurt (or thinks so) feels unnecessary, begins to doubt the rest and, of course, himself, and at the end his interaction with society becomes difficult and problematic.

In other words, if someone alone offended a person, he would constantly wind himself up and behave worse and worse in relation to other people. Where does jealousy come from?

This feeling has several sources. It may arise due to resentment in the past.

Apparently, a person from the past was promised something and forgot, or simply deceived. And now this person wants to know, understand and make sure that he will not be deceived again?

It is worth noting that our people are met in the world and such people for whom there are only two concepts, "either all or nothing." That is, if they are not the best, then they are necessarily the worst. This problem becomes especially acute when such people begin to suspect that their half are sympathetic to someone else. If a person does not choose them, they are angry and hate the whole world. And, as a rule, loneliness becomes the next source of jealousy. If a person feels bad, feels fear and pain due to the fact that he considers himself lonely, he will undoubtedly be jealous of other people if they spend their time not with him. Does jealousy have any kind?

Jealousy is a complex feeling. But to calculate the types or types of it is very simple. Just look at the actions of a jealous person. If he takes care and cares for another person, his life and health, then his actions will say: "You are dear to me." Because of the fear of losing something, people are trying to control other people. Unfortunately, sometimes such control hurts others, and even serious problems like violence happen. Here is such a rapid development from concern for injuries shows a thin line between healthy and not quite jealousy.

Psychotherapy expert W. Frankl argues that jealousy is stupid and a mistake. She may not be justified if the partner is faithful. Or justified if he cheats. But in the second case, it is meaningless, since such a relationship is a failure. Jealousy is a dangerous feeling. Man is actually afraid of losing love. And at the same time, he himself leads to such a loss with his constant suspicions and distrust.

If there were losses in a person's life, he was deceived and betrayed; one should not live with resentment against the others. After all, this will lead to the same losses only in a larger amount.

To avoid losses from jealousy, you just need to stop cheating yourself, think about your inferiority, and, most importantly, trust other people.

Codependency and counter-dependence

Why does a counter-dependent person at the beginning of a relationship behave as a co-dependent, exhibiting characteristic features of him? What is the essence of this situation?

You meet a person, he is fully involved in your relationship, giving them all their free time and completely himself - constant meetings and walks, intensive correspondence in instant messengers, joint plans. This is one of the signs of a codependent relationship. Then, at some point, the person "merges", chopping off all the contacts, and at best, sometimes appears in your life or completely disappears for a long time. After some time, he returns, continuing to build relationships according to an already familiar scenario - constantly nearby, correspondence, miss, love, I can't live, etc. In general, this is a fairly standard behavior of a counter-dependent person.

However, an inexplicable feeling of duality remains - on the one hand, counter-dependent behavior, and on the other - co-dependent. Why it happens?

The thing is that the essence of counter-dependent and codependent behavior is the same - dependence! This is an emotional addiction, failure at the level of attachment. And this failure occurs approximately the same way - both in the codependent person and in the counter-dependent person. The only difference is that the co-dependent person does not feel himself without the other, therefore, clutching for a partner (he cannot feed himself, see the colors of life, and indeed - he has nothing to enjoy in life if there is no other nearby). Often such people even wake up lifeless if they have to fall asleep alone.

With regard to the counter-dependent personality, a slightly different picture of the world. A counter-dependent person is a person dependent on his independence. Relatively speaking, he has such a huge love for his freedom (dependent and painful) that relations for such a person are simply unbearable, cause inconvenience, pain and some kind of rejection. This interferes with both his personal life and internal. How were both of these characters formed?

The basis here is common - the lack of a fairly strong emotional connection with the mother, conditionally-point attachment, when the mother left for a long time, and the child did not understand whether she would return at all. In general, this is a lack of emotional contact from the mother.

For example, in childhood, a person had a nanny, and his mother was included in his life only an hour a day, but she did not have emotional trauma in the attachment zone (the failure was clearly there, but not so deep, it was possible to correct the situation in just a few sessions)

So, the issue of emotional contact with the mother figure is of fundamental and important importance here. Did mom notice my needs? Have you noticed changes in the expression on my face? Have you seen that I don't like it, I don't want it (I don't want to eat it, I don't want to wear it), but I want it - buy it to me, please! Did she hear me? Did you agree with me?

Codependency is formed a little earlier than counter-dependence - approximately at the age of a year and a half, when the child had to separate from the mother earlier than he was ready for it (taken to the kindergarten or began to give more often to his grandmother, etc.). Accordingly, the baby has become much less likely to see his mother, which was very critical for him and, as a result, there was a deep-seated inner need "mother, don't leave, please let me hug you." This is a picture when a child holds on to his mother's foot and asks tearfully: "Mom! Do not leave! "

A similar situation is imprinted in the psyche, as a way of attachment and in adulthood. What is the difference between counter-dependence?

 A counter-dependent character is formed on the basis of the excessive involvement of the mother's figure - sadistic care, mother's hyperocclusion, but not in the emotional life of the child, but rather in the functional (put on a hat; eat even more, otherwise you ate very little; you did not wear boots; you don't cold, etc.).

Relatively speaking, a mother knows for a child what exactly he needs. The most important aspect is a gross violation of the child's emotional boundaries (he is not allowed to be alone with himself, although he really wants to).

In fact, in which zone the child will go - to co-dependence or counter-dependence - in the absence of important factors of emotional connection with the mother and insufficient merging with her at an earlier age, depends on the structure of the psyche of the child with whom he was born (a person may be sensitive from birth , and maybe more thick-skinned). Given a more sensitive and vulnerable child and, accordingly, a similar strong violation of borders by parents or people raising him, he is more likely to go into counterdependency.

So, if there was an excessive violation of boundaries on the part of the parental figures, the child was not allowed to retire, having matured, he would choose the position of loneliness, since for him the relationship is excessive tension, some kind of pain, the need to get involved where he is not interested in being. His emotional sphere is not included in this zone, because he was not directly included in it in childhood.

A counter-dependent type can be formed even if the family had incomprehensible relationships between adults. For example, mom and dad constantly find out relations between themselves, scandals, abuse and beatings, and the child joins in this ("Dad, don't beat mom!", "Mom, leave dad alone!"), Each time choosing between parents. In this case, the relationship for him became a strain of such a level that the muscles are shaking, because the psyche of the kids is very small, and he has to contain a huge amount of stress in the family.

Another option is a quarrel between dad and mother-in-law or mother and mother-in-law, and all these disassemblies have always occurred in front of the child. Maybe the situation is different - the child did not see anything, but the mother, father or other relative close to his heart complained using the baby as a "container" ("Your mom or dad are like that ..."). As a result, the child loves everyone equally, splits up inside his consciousness, experiencing enormous stress and trying to keep his psyche in order not to go into psychosis. Subsequently, having matured, this person will see the relationship as too stressful. In addition, he can automatically get involved in the problems of his partner, start solving them, receiving very high stress from this. However, the instinctive need for fusion, warm emotional contact, and secure attachment remains with the counter-dependent person. With age, our entire human being will nonetheless draw us to other people, because all people are social beings.

That is why such a person insanely and sincerely wants to have a relationship, he goes to them, meeting a partner with whom he merges, but an internal conflict does not allow him to set boundaries on time. The American psychologist Barry Weinhold has books on counterdependency and codependency - "Escape from intimacy" and "Liberation from codependency", respectively. " It is better to read them at the same time, because quite often from the outside it seems that a person is counter-dependent, but inside he experiences himself as co-dependent (and vice versa).

Both codependent and counterdependent individuals have other dependencies besides emotional (for example, alcohol, drugs, pills, diets, sports, work, adrenaline addiction).

If a person goes in for sports more than three times a week, this is already a dependency (the exception is professional sports), and there is a strong violation in the psyche zone (relatively speaking, without physical exertion, a person feels unwell, and depression constantly prevails in his mood).

Any dependence implies the fact that a person has no boundaries, self-sensitivity (when enough, and when not), in other words, a person does not know how to survive an aversion to excessiveness (this is like a "buffet", when everything offered is eaten at one moment and then ill and sick). Accordingly, he merges into a relationship, "eats" everything that is offered to him (time, emotions, worries, events, walks, love-carrots), gets poisoned and leaves, not understanding why he suddenly became ill.

Another important point in the context of this problem is the fear of being absorbed in a partner. Experiencing a panic state of anxiety, a person turns off other feelings, and an aversion to excessiveness occurs only when "everything eaten begins to fall out of the mouth." As a rule, this leads to the fact that people get a little lost, then calm down, disgust gradually disappears, and they can again return to the relationship.

So, a person cannot limit and stop himself, and this is directly related to his early relationship with his mother. At the age of 1-3 years, the child begins to set restrictions (for example, you have 5 candies, but you can eat only 1, etc.), and the baby is upset, frustrated, cries and screams, resents his parents and manipulates, but the parent must set a clear line at this place.

Another situation - the baby plays with his toys, mom (dad, grandmother, grandfather) enters the room and demands to remove the toys, motivating this at a later time ("We remove the toys, it's time to sleep, it's already 9 o'clock in the evening! Play it later, now sleep!"). In this case, the child's boundaries are violated, he feels that relations are a connection that frustrates, violates his freedom, will, blocks his desire and emotional sphere. A deep ligament remains in the child's mind, the belief is formed that relations are bad, and everyone needs to be saved, to be a container. Such a firm opinion can only be changed only by gaining new experience in relationships, when no one is above you, does not command, does not say where to go and what to do is the experience of psychotherapy.

You may be lucky with a partner and he will not violate your borders, but there may be a reverse situation - you will provoke him to violate your borders, to swallow you, and then, accordingly, blame him for everything ("You swallow me up! "). In fact, your child's psyche reproduces childhood experiences with parents because you couldn't tell your mother: "It's your fault, you offended me, you did this ..." Thoughts may have been expressed aloud, but it didn't lead to anything, and your command has not changed.

Other factors can also be at the heart of the problem - the specific situation, certain actions of the parents, on which your appropriate behavior has been included. As a rule, several recurring events, relationships, etc. become the cause of the injury. The difficulty lies in the fact that the period from a year to three years is quite difficult to remember, and many people do not remember this age. Depending on human behavior, only ligaments can be found.

Irritation, anger, anger and rage

How is anger felt and what to do with it?

The spectrum of anger is quite large - at first we feel dissatisfaction, then irritation, then anger, then anger and rage.

Anger and rage is not so much a feeling as an affect. Affect is an emotional state, short-term, but saturated in intensity, which is very difficult to control, almost impossible. But anger itself is a feeling, and it can be controlled. Dissatisfaction is felt like a worm sitting inside and saying that something is wrong. Irritation is felt like itching, not even so much on the body as on the inside. There is a desire to shove everyone, but not with a storm of emotions, but just a feeling that everything is not right and everything is wrong, everyone does not like it. Anger is already felt as a stronger and more concentrated state of irritation. If irritation could be felt throughout the body, then anger is concentrated in the chest and arms. And we understand that we already strongly dislike what is happening.

Anger is an indication that people are advancing on our borders. That is, they violate our comfortable distance with another person.

For example, if we are used to the fact that certain things in our house lie in a certain place, then if someone puts them in another place, then this can cause us anger. Just a feeling of anger. What shall we do next with this anger is our choice. At this stage, we can still choose.

With feelings of dissatisfaction, irritation and anger, we still have the opportunity to choose what to do with them, but with anger and rage it is already more difficult. Anger can be more or less held back. You can feel that someone or someone's actions are already furious, but still hold on. Anger is felt more in the hands than anger. Hands burn directly and you want to do something with them (for example, to hit, or many people start cleaning in this state or any other actions so that their hands are involved)

In a state of rage, it is impossible to hold feelings. In this state, there is a lot of energy, the body has a feeling that everything is burning, sometimes you want to run, go, do something, throw, scream. If we allowed anger to become rage, then we are unlikely to be able to restrain it.

With feelings of dissatisfaction, irritation and anger, we still have the opportunity to make a choice what to do with them. There are two opposite patterns of behavior (now I bring two extremes).

The first model of behavior is to immediately splash out all the emotions that come (this is what fellow psychoanalysts call acting out). Then everyone around us suffers, then often people turn away from us. And there is a model of behavior when a person does not tell the world anything about his feelings of anger and leaves his anger in himself (perhaps out of fear that everything will turn its back on us if we splash out all our emotions, as in the first case). The anger that goes into us goes into our body, and can be presented to us in the form of a disease. Or this anger can manifest itself as auto-aggressive behavior.

Auto-aggressive behavior - when we are angry with someone, but we hold ourselves so as not to express our anger to this someone, and instead direct the anger in a different way towards ourselves (this can be frequent innocent bodily harm, for example, a person is often hit it starts - either on a chair, then on a table, then on a bed, then burns, then gets into a situation where he could be harmed, and so on, it can be different destructive behavior in relation to himself - up to thoughts or attempts of suicide)

With auto-aggressive behavior, as a rule, we are angry with someone, but this someone is such a kind, good, nice person, he has done so much good for us that we simply cannot afford to be angry with him. And so we turn our entire anger on ourselves. A more balanced model of behavior is when, first of all, we try to understand what exactly made us angry and look deeper. Not a cup that has not been washed for 10 days makes us angry, but the fact that the partner does not devote time to us and does not value all that we do for him, for example.

Next comes the thought process - what would we like in this situation, what would we not want, what other feelings does this situation arouse in us? What unmet needs lie behind our anger?

There is always an unmet need for anger. Then a sincere conversation with a partner (well, or with a person who was angry with us), in which we talk about our feelings when he does or does not do such-and-such, and our request to do so-and-so.

I emphasize once again, we are talking specifically about feelings, not passing on to insults, not going over, as they say to a person. This is possible if you start this dialogue, not when anger is on the verge of anger or rage. This is possible after a while, after the feelings have settled down a bit. We listen to his counterarguments, trying to understand what kind of feelings he (she) is experiencing in connection with the topic raised. The technique is quite difficult to describe, since there are many nuances. Each of us needs personal experience to understand how this works for each of us. The main thing here is to understand each other's feelings, pains in this situation. And give the right to another person to disagree with you. And it is important to agree on how we will interact with each other in the next similar situation so that no one is hurt.

In the Gestalt approach, it is believed that the feeling does not lie, that it is the truth, and behind it one can find a true need, not shrouded in bonds of socialization or obligation.

Therefore, when we speak with others in the language of feelings (that is, we show the other person not that he is bad, because this or that, but that you feel offended because the other did this or that), we become understandable, and another can hear us, because our words do not offend him.

In addition, I believe that one should not be afraid sometimes and have a row with one another. This releases a lot of energy into contact, including positive. More precisely, this allows the emergence of positive feelings in a relationship. Indeed, through conflict, through anger to another and a constructive exit - is true closeness in a relationship.

When we run the risk of being angry with another, when we find ourselves accepted by another, even evil, this gives rise to even more

trust in the partner, which means even more warm and tender feelings
afterwards.

The mechanism for the development of love addiction

Love addiction is a state in which one person falls in love or becomes
very attached to another, practically living his life (all thoughts are
fixated on the object of adoration, and the worst thing is that he is
panicky afraid of losing it). As a rule, behind this line of behavior hides
an early trauma of attachment. A child who was left at an early age to be
raised by grandparents; between children in the family a little age
difference; the mother worked a lot - such situations ultimately cause a
trauma of attachment and an insane fear of losing her partner. This
feeling is so chilling and absorbing that a person is ready to completely
abandon himself and his Self. He controls the partner in everything, he
can even just walk on his heels and whimper tearfully: "Just don't leave
me! You are welcome!". How does love addiction develop?

At the first stage, a person has an all-consuming feeling of infinite
happiness, wings "grow", each meeting with a lover / lover brings an
additional portion of euphoria, an incredible emotional outburst that
lifts him to the "seventh heaven".

The second stage consists of two parts - the expectation of a meeting in a
state of sweet euphoria and excitement; an unstoppable desire to prolong
a date as long as possible. Usually people with a love addiction can be on
a date for 10-12 hours, until late at night or in the morning - they can not
part with a partner and let him go on vacation.

At the third stage, the dependent person begins to understand that
reality does not coincide with the expected and desired image of the
partner - he does not reach the ideal, speaks wrong, puts on the wrong

clothes, etc. As a result, annoying reproaches and empty nit-picking begin. At the fourth stage, unsuccessful attempts to change the partner appear. Here you need to remember that another person can only change if he has a sufficient degree of motivation and a well-developed resistance. Against the background of all these events, the addicted person has increased nervousness, because his whole life is focused exclusively on the object of affection. There is a feeling of guilt due to my failure - "I can't change my partner! So, I'm doing something wrong, and the reason is in me! " Fear of losing a loved one is associated with desire (a real partner is still imperfect, but somewhere there is an ideal and desired partner). The origins of this behavior are related to childhood - the age of 3-5 years, when the child deidealizes his parent (for example, mom / dad can not always buy everything I want, or stop the rain).

Thus, the person remained in the merger period, was unable to separate from his parents at the right time, and, accordingly, he lives on the eternal idealization with each next partner. Sometimes unbridled anger may arise, a person begins to take revenge on a partner for the fact that he is imperfect.

So, at this stage there is de-idealization, disappointment and depreciation. There may also be a burning causeless hatred, control and a desperate attempt to still change a partner, up to tyranny. In fact, the addicted person feels very bad - a state of nervousness does not allow him to rest normally, he cannot sleep at all, unable to think of anything other than his partner.

All his actions are connected with the fact that a very early trauma of attachment related to the maternal object was affected - there was not enough merging and idealization of the mother, the child did not receive comfort when he was upset and disappointed by something, maybe he did not have time to be charmed (born and he immediately had to become an adult; his parents or educators rejected him, not allowing him to be small, to make mistakes and fall, to speak incorrectly; they demanded more from him than he could do at his age, etc.).

As a result, a person in adulthood behaves similarly with attachment objects, suffering greatly from such behavior (neurosis, internal self-flagellation, complete deprivation from the world, obsessive thoughts like Walker (obsessive-compulsive disorder), lack of interest in anything else etc.).

Sometimes a person lives in a cycle of obsessed thoughts and failed plans - what will happen when we see each other; what will he tell me; what will i do. After a few days, additional memories pop up in my mind, and the cycle "starts" again - he told me so, and I definitely had to answer like this.

Such a state for a person with love addiction is so destructive that even love addiction was made as a disease!

Myths about true love

Many people who cannot build strong and stable relationships over a long period of time are not able to choose a partner, make a mature decision about marriage and start a family, they simply not only have no experience of healthy relationships, but they have not seen them in your life.

As a rule, they observed the behavior of parents in a divorce or family quarrel.

There may be another situation - each parent was engaged exclusively in his own life, the family did not have common interests. Accordingly, the child is not able to understand the questions: What kind of relationship do parents have? How did they meet? Do they love each other, because outwardly no relationship is noticeable at all?

From the side of the parental relationship, the whole conscious life of the child looked ideal, but when he was 15-20 years old, for some reason they divorced. Or the clarification of the relationship between father and mother always happened quietly and behind a closed door, so the child could not figure out what and why happened.

So, what happens at this stage with the internal state of a person? He tries to compensate for the lack of visual experience with information from various sources - as a rule, these are love stories (Cinderella, fairy tales about beautiful princesses, etc.) and romantic American films with a happy ending. However, real happiness requires hard work, so that your life becomes more realistic and happier, you need to understand the myths of true love and debunk them.

True love is always love at first sight. In general, today this myth is almost debunked - each of us has come across people who fell in love with their future partner not the second or even the third time.

There are such situations that love occurs when a person is, it would seem, in a long and stable relationship with another partner, or he could see and appreciate his only one only after some time after meeting.

It is important to remember that some people need a lot of time so that deep down they can completely relax and then trust another person. Only after complete inner reassurance can they say: "Yes, I love this man!"

Nowadays, there are quite a lot of people in the world with various deep injuries (especially with attachment injuries), therefore it is impossible to trust in a split second. On the contrary, quite often there are situations when relationships that began with crazy love at first sight just as quickly and fade away. Why it happens?

In fact, this is idealization and depreciation of the partner, but in reality there is no strong and deep affection and sincere love. It may be that people fall in love at first sight, but then they work long and hard on their relationship, cultivating their love step by step, constantly moving towards each other and finding out the most hidden thoughts. A period of disappointment passes, a period of irritation - and true love comes.

Most people still believe in the "theory of halves." This is a fabulous myth that once upon a time each of us was physically connected with our partner, but then there was a terrible catastrophe that divided us. Since then, all people "wander" around the world in search of their soul mates. However, if this were so, until now people simply could not meet their partner, fall in love and have a family.

Today, the World Wide Web gives an unlimited number of options to find love all over the world - dating sites and various chat rooms allow you to chat with people from Canada, Austria, New Zealand, America, etc. If a person is destined for fate, a single partner will surely be able to find him; but if there wasn't the Internet, the couple wouldn't be able to reunite.

Alas, this wonderful theory is false. Each person independently makes a decision about his mission in life and chooses a mate. Nothing has been written anywhere about who will be your soulmate - neither God nor the Universe. It is important to understand that we ourselves choose the partner to which our soul responds.

Do not set an overwhelming task - to consider, relatively speaking, God's intention. Accept responsibility for your choice, find a person who is good enough for yourself and build strong relationships. The object of love is the one and only person. This is from the category of idealization and depreciation - you must find the ideal person who will suit you in everything and arrange at every point. You will never swear and conflict with him, there will be no anger at each other.

Firstly, you simply will not allow yourself to show similar feelings towards your loved one, and secondly, if the partner gets angry for something, you will have a firm belief that the closest person has stopped loving you. This opinion is erroneous. Love and anger are inseparable companions, and this is quite normal.

If in relations with your partner you at least occasionally do not feel anger, then there is no relationship. A partner may be with flaws in character, you may be annoyed in response to some of his actions, disappointed. It is important that you are comfortable and pleasant to be with this person. Relatively speaking, more than 50% of the time spent with a loved one should not be a burden for you.

If this is not the case, do not specifically deify the partner or get stuck in a showdown, when you generally look in different directions and completely do not understand each other. Look around and find a person with whom you will be really comfortable and calm in any situation.

So, if you have been trying for some time to sort things out, try to find a common language with your partner, but you see that everyone has their own opinion, this is an indicator that your one and only ceased to be like that.

The story of eternal love is a romantic tale of Cinderella, American melodramas, stories that end with "and they lived happily ever after." However, no one tells how long and happily the heroes lived, how their happiness looked - this is clearly not a frozen picture in the form of a kiss on the whole screen. Life implies dynamics and different feelings, experiences, events and meetings - this is normal.

Unlimited self-sacrifice, renunciation of one's own interests.
This is probably one of the most terrible myths, although many people are now addicted to psychology and psychotherapy. To give up yourself and become a victim is quite dangerous. Often we don't notice how relationships completely absorb us, taking all our free time and making us our humble slave (we stopped meeting friends, put off our hobbies, didn't read for a long time, forgot about our favorite food, do not watch movies, etc.).

As a rule, in a pair, partners stop monitoring themselves - malnutrition, bad habits. Basically, all this happens unconsciously (especially if you are addicted to addictive behavior and addiction).

At the very beginning of the relationship, people are merged and exhibit a codependent behavior model (even if in fact they are counter-dependent).

Observe yourself; analyze the moments in which you lose yourself as a person, where you follow the partner, not understanding your personal desires and not including awareness and energy. All these points are very important. Why?

Most often, relationships in which partners sacrifice themselves in order to "be together" quickly disintegrate, ending at the "boy-girl" stage. In addition, people begin to suffer from various psychosomatic diseases - losing ourselves in a relationship, we lose not only our body, but also life as a whole.

The reverse situation is that a person lives in a world of illusion ("Everything is wonderful in a relationship. We are so similar, we like the same things, we do everything together. I no longer love my friends, I don't need them! Yes, and I don't have a hobby for a long time the only thing that really interests me is what are you doing? Let's do it together! "Such a strong merger in a pair leads to complete and unforgivable blindness of the partners to each other. Finally, insight comes when a person finds out that the partner is big part of the relationship cheated on him. Love needs to be earned.

For example, in the post-Soviet countries, a way of thinking that maximum suffering forms true and great love is rooted. The mentality of people or those who have grown up / been born in a distant USSR implies a sacrificial behavior pattern - they completely forget about themselves and completely surrender to other people.Accordingly, if I suffered all these feelings, it means that love is real; otherwise, in a relationship something is wrong. that erroneous belief that a good guy who does not drink, does not smoke and decently earns, does not physically attract a woman. And only experiencing a derogatory attitude towards herself (including domestic violence), she is convinced that they love her. The world around is quite narcissistic, so if we don't do something for another person, we won't be good enough for him, we won't be loved.

In principle, all adult relationships are built on the basis of these beliefs, and this is normal. However, the opinion "they will not love me" becomes so important and priority that a person forgets about himself as a person.

As a result, there is a stalemate situation - if a person in a relationship tries to adapt to his partner, he will not be able to love and respect him.

To deserve love with suffering also does not work - no one likes to bring pain to another person (if both partners are not psychopaths).

Love is salvation from loneliness. It is unbearable for a man to be alone, so he tries to find a partner so that it is not so scary.

As a rule, the whole depth of this belief is not realized by our consciousness.

True love is equal to quality sex by default. Great sex the first time - partners are perfect for each other. Alas, good sexual contact the first time is very rare today, especially for those who have not been in a relationship for a long time. Our neural connections are used to having fun in a certain way, and changing the script will affect the nature of the orgasm.

Accordingly, big and pure love does not always mean quality sex at once. At least a year is needed for grinding in sexual relations, and only after that we can judge whether the partners are suitable for each other sexually. In addition, it is a turbulent sexual experience in a relationship that testifies more to passion than to love. Strong arousal and attraction (up to madness) covers us only in relation to destructive personalities that are completely unsuitable for relationships.

For a long and stable relationship you need quiet and calm love. However, this does not mean that the level of passion for a partner should be at "zero", it is quite average. True love - positive and joyful feelings, always euphoria and mutual understanding.

If there is any negative attitude towards the partner, this phenomenon is short-term and quickly passes. In order to pass the negative in relation to the partner, the couple needs to communicate more, to understand the needs of everyone.

A long and stable relationship is not one hundred percent pleasure. For about 5 years (from the second to the seventh year of relations), the partners arrange a showdown, criticize each other, distance themselves, become disappointed and annoyed in everyone's actions. But even at a distance, and distancing emotionally, people can continue to love each other.

Feverish euphoria and a constant feeling of "butterflies and rainbows" in the stomach do not at all speak of normal and sincere feelings of partners.

How to understand that this is your man

Quite often they offer a simple way - to rely solely on your feelings (I love, I can't live without him). However, such statements are mostly neurotic desires.

A person who has had some kind of trauma or a difficult relationship in the family during his childhood (for example, an alcoholic father, a victim mother, daffodil parents, a cold maternal figure) will enter into relationships with people similar to parents - thus the psyche trying to close this trauma, open gestalt, to change something in that distant childhood situation.

Our psyche does not know that this is impossible, accordingly, at such moments various neurotic desires appear. Strong marriages are often based on the financial benefit of partners, in general on comfort (people are comfortable sharing life, they interact well with each other) and on friendship (partners communicate a lot and understand each other) and do not rest on an emotional boom, but on lowered tones.

As a rule, in such families relations are reliable, everything is calm and there is no heat of passion. In those relations where there are violent passions, there is a downside - a lot of resentment, frustration, anger, misunderstanding, jealousy.

So, how to determine that the man with whom you are now in a relationship, really suits you?

Remember that all of the symptoms listed below are quite subjective. Assessing the situation is worth about a year of relations. The first joint year or several months, everything will be wonderful, you are in a merger with a partner - this is quite normal, without this relationship may not work out. However, if you can distance yourself a little emotionally from a person and look at relationships from the side, it is important to be able to really evaluate them. You have no doubt that this is your man, he suits you for who he is. You are able to accept it right now with all its shortcomings (and it is very surprising here that you are reading a similar article!).

If you are wondering, "Is this man suitable for me?", "Is this my man?", "How to understand that your man?" - This is an indicator that you have doubts. Of course, in the modern world we always have a choice - to stay in a relationship or break up, divorce is possible at any time. Think about the extent of your doubts?

Relatively speaking, how much interest do you doubt, how much more bad than good is in your relationship?

Positive points should be at least a few percent more, and this already gives you a reason to stay with this man. It is very important to be able to accept other people for who they are, and for this, learn to accept yourself first. When you can accept yourself with all the shortcomings ("Yes, I am so, it's not always nice, but I'm such a person"), allow yourself to be imperfect, then you can accept imperfection and your partner. You are comfortable next to this person, he attracts you physically. Smell, body, skin do not cause disgust and rejection.

Sometimes there are situations when you do not want physical intimacy and tenderness at all, but in general, his body is pleasant to you, and you do not pull your hand when touched. This option does not apply to first dates - during this period you may be uncomfortable when a stranger still touches you. If you have been familiar for some time, are close, touch should not cause discomfort. You are generally calm and comfortable next to a man, it's easy to talk with him, open your soul, talk about yourself. In response, you feel acceptance - he listens carefully to you, he is interested to be near you.

An important nuance - if you feel uncomfortable in something, analyze the situation, figure out why it is the feeling of lack of comfort next to a loved one. I can't do it myself - I need therapy, one consultation will be enough to reveal the weaknesses of the relationship.

Take a closer look at your partner - is he comfortable next to you? Is he open to communication? Does the man really say what he wants, or adapts to the thread of your dialogue? If a person constantly hides his opinion, adapting on the go to a conversation, this is, relatively speaking, the effect of a compressed spring. At some point, it will burst sharply, and relations will change dramatically, up to a break in a pair. Noticed such behavior, be sure to talk with your partner - it is important that he, too, is comfortable and cozy in relations with you. You don't have the feeling that he should deserve me. You feel that this man is worthy of you right now - the way he is (with all the shortcomings and advantages).

Learn to build relationships without requirements - no one owes anything to anyone. A partner can brighten up your life, but he should not. You feel that he understands you and accepts as you are now, does not discuss and does not criticize.

Sometimes situations may arise when a partner makes a remark to you, tries to indicate your behavior, but these statements do not hurt you, do not hurt you. In relationships, this nuance is very important - a person who always tries to hurt you, spoils your self-esteem, traumatizes you, and eventually your couple breaks up. The constant criticism of the partner, his discontent, the desire to change you, to rebuild the relationship as he wants, will not bring any benefit. Your plans for the future, life goals and values coincide - for example, both of you want to live outside the city (or in the city center), you want children (or vice versa). This implies things that are directly related to your life together, and to make them yourself is quite difficult.

Nowadays, many people are in a relationship, but do not live together (this is the so-called "guest marriage"). If it is important for your partner to share a common territory, you cannot be together. Another example - bodily contact with a loved one is extremely important for you, but he loves to sleep alone and cannot stand tenderness. Paired with you will be quite difficult with this person.

That is why at the very beginning of the relationship it is very important to clarify all the nuances, understand the joint plans, evaluate each other's vision, life values. Do not console yourself with vain illusions - we will get married, go deeper into relationships, and I will certainly change his point of view ("Let's do it like me!", "Let's live outside the city!"). You will not be able to do this, but it would seem that "successful attempts" will only lead to growing tension within the family - the partner will suffer, show passive discontent, and in general will be unhappy in relations.

In the matter of choosing a partner, it is important not only to evaluate the person, but also to understand what is happening between you - how you agree, how you relate to each other's pain, whether you hear each other, whether you can share some intimate experiences, tell about your injuries (how childhood passed, for which they scolded what moments left a painful imprint in the mind), to accept each other with this pain, injuries, features and deficiencies.

In a relationship, you need to be able to hear, understand, negotiate, give in or compromise. Ask yourself - how is this happening with you? Maybe you are never ready to compromise, and the partner is always ready to adjust, and in contact you both are quite comfortable, calm and comfortable.

All of the listed signs are rather ambiguous, and are not suitable for all pairs. There are partners who constantly swear, quarrel, beat dishes, shout - and live like this for years! From the outside there is a feeling that they hate each other, but if they are separated at least for a day, they will be bored.

There are also situations where people live in a pair of very old age, and when one of the partners dies, the second very soon follows him (although in life they could live "like a cat and a dog"). It happens differently - outwardly it seems that the partners live quietly, even at home the atmosphere is calm, they do not swear and have a nice conversation, but in reality with close communication it turns out that there is no relationship for a long time, and all this time people lived together for the sake of children.

First of all, be sure to rely on yourself, your feelings, comfort / discomfort. If your relationship does not match according to many criteria (cursing, often painfully, uncomfortable with a partner), but you feel that something is holding you next to this person, stay in the relationship. This is an occasion for you to develop your psyche, study your psychology, understand yourself and understand what injuries are holding you in these relationships.

Relations are always development, they point us to those areas that need to be worked out. If you really want to stay in a relationship, then you really need it.

Work on yourself, and maybe the relationship will change, you will change - in any case, it will be for the better. Feel that you need this - do not get hung up on any criteria, go and work on relationships and yourself.

Whether to leave the partner

Why can one of the partners toss between the choice to leave the partner or stay? What to do in this case?

In fact, such a phenomenon is not uncommon - many people come to personal consultations with a similar request. And here it is worth exploring in more detail. Sometimes a person can change several partners, but all the time stepping on the same rake, he constantly becomes very uncomfortable in a relationship.

The reason is either different each time, or the same one, but he cannot cope with it on his own, therefore he breaks up his relationship and suffers, first experiencing grief from the breakup, and then doubts and fears in finding a new partner. However, the point is not in the partner himself, but in what happens to such a person inside.

Two main factors can be distinguished - such people are characterized by some kind of counter-dependence, or they are so unconsciously separated from their parents. They don't have the feeling that separation from the parental figures happened, so trying to separate from the partner, they seem to say to their consciousness: "Look, I was able to get away from him!" So, what influences the emergence of such doubts in one of the partners?

This is often pain associated with the fact that relationships bring more tension than pleasure and relaxation. The origins must be sought in childhood - perhaps in the family people received more negativity (insults, humiliation, condemnation, the person was not accepted for who he is). And then in adult relationships he has to strain hard, play someone else's role for himself. Breaking relationships and leaving your partner will not close your deep need to relax, in trust, acceptance, recognition, comfort in relationships, so that they are calm and cozy.

All of these needs are very difficult to realize for an injured person in a real relationship. What to do in such cases?

The best option is psychotherapy. It is impossible to change this type of character in any other way. Why?

All other options are so unstable that they will not provide you with security in relationships, and this is the basic need of a person with a similar character and trauma (the partner with whom you are building a relationship must be completely emotionally safe so that you can be trusted, and accessible at least once a week at the appointed time)

There are people who, not having separated from their parents, went into a codependent relationship - they find a partner, cling to him and live like that. There is another category - those who are comfortable being next to another person, but not with themselves.

The last option is people acting out a counterscript against any addiction model (in this case, they perceive attachment as something terrible, they are afraid of merging with a partner, absorption - as a close person themselves, and vice versa). These fears are so deep that it is simply impossible to build close relationships. As a rule, a strong desire to leave a partner arises at times when the relationship becomes closer (something happened in the pair, and you realized that the partner perceives you as you really are - and after you realize the whole situation, you have strong desire to run away) - I'd rather run away, because there is a big danger that I can fall in love completely and become dependent on him, relax, let my inner child go outside, and then this person will hurt me. In fact, this belief is very unconscious. Outwardly, people with similar psychological problems look very independent ("I can do everything myself! I don't need anyone!"), But as soon as everyone disagrees and they are alone, a tantrum begins ("No, I need people! We need those who can withstand me, can be with me! ").

And here different checks may appear, and border acting out - to leave the partner to see if he will return, whether he will run after him.

It is important to understand that the root of the problem is exclusively within you and is connected with your parents. Why can everything be changed only in therapy sessions?

Only after receiving an internal, in-depth experience of other relationships, you can transfer this to your personal life and not be so afraid of intimacy. Closeness in therapy develops very slowly - in small steps, it can be paused, control the distance with the therapist.

Good therapists are very careful about people with an avoidant personality type, with counterdependency, do not violate their boundaries. Regardless of the type of character (in life, a person can be choleric and very active), some psychological processes they take much longer, especially in relation to proximity.

Relatively speaking, trauma is a "stop" of our psyche at some point in development. Counterdependence is the moment of development at the age of 3 years, the earliest period when the first separation should occur. For some reason, separation from the parental figures did not happen or was rather painful and sharp, as a result, the child retreated into himself, having decided that he would not become attached to anyone.

There are many options for the development of this situation, but there is only one result - a person is removed from proximity, although he really wants to experience it. That is why, if you have met such a person in a relationship, make an effort on yourself and let him move at a pace that is acceptable to him. Do not put pressure on your partner, let your closeness form slowly, then it will be true closeness.

What to do if the husband is often angry

Unfortunately, no one taught us at school how to react to rudeness, aggression and insults. Spouse aggression is a really sore subject, but how should one respond in order to preserve one's dignity?

First, pay attention to how it is customary to communicate in the family of the spouse. Perhaps a rude attitude towards each other ("What are you doing? Sit down and calm down. Why are you aching?") Is the norm. This is a kind of "affection" for relatives. In this case, changing this behavior is quite difficult, it will take a lot of time. Sometimes the roots of ill-treatment are still so deep that a different style of communication in this family is simply unacceptable, so be prepared for the worst outcome — breaking the relationship.

If everyone in your family is talking to each other with warmth and love, bring your husband more often to yourself. It is likely that he will resist, he will not like this idea (even though it is better). A man will clearly understand that this style of communication is much more comfortable. But his psyche will feel fear and hostility towards all kind people, it will seem to him that in the end all this will not lead to anything good. Ask yourself - what can you do?

Cultivate your spouse with love, affection and tenderness. However, you will have to be much stronger, smarter, wiser and more mature than him. Try to answer each rudeness kindly, say that you generally understand his situation: "Yes, I understand that it is customary in your family to communicate like this, but let's try to talk differently, I feel uncomfortable in such a moral environment. It hurts me. "

Always talk with your spouse, say that you do not like this style of communication ("Please do not talk to me like that!", "Could you say this in a softer tone?").

Do the exercises, but not at the moment when the husband got angry. Learn to distinguish in which cases the anger is real and in which the evil phrase just "flies out" on the machine due to the fact that this was customary in his family. If the spouse is really angry, it's better not to get into conversations. Let the emotional outburst pass, the man will calm down, only then you can talk about what you didn't like ("Let's you and I do the simple exercise" Try to say differently. "Why am I causing you such anger? What can I do, so you don't get angry? ").

It is very important that the communication is two-way - you must also see, realize and accept your guilt. If only he is guilty of the fact that the husband is angry, the situation will become tense, causing even greater aggression and anger on his part. A man will openly confront you. That is why you need to take some of the blame on yourself ("Good. What are my actions that made you angry now?").

Do not manipulate your spouse's emotions by saying what he wants to hear.

Work on yourself honestly, because in a good way your contribution to his emotional state is also there. Do not take spouse aggression at your own expense.

If your husband, in principle, is characterized by rudeness and aggressive behavior (for example, this is a temperamental man, choleric), accept this feature of his character. Remember that aggressiveness, arousal, and sexuality always go hand in hand. Thus, by killing aggression in a spouse, you can simply kill sexual relationships.

Relationships are the hard work of both partners. In certain situations, try to accept and recognize the spouse's aggressive tone, find a compromise, explain to your husband that he, too, can try to reduce his emotional tension. But the most important thing is to understand that you didn't necessarily do something bad, don't try to radically change your behavior, don't be ashamed of your appearance, character and, in general, yourself, as a person.

In most cases, the husband just wants to tell you something by his behavior. If you tried many times to talk with your husband, change him with your affection and kindness, or accept your partner as he is, but you did not succeed, then you do not have enough kindness! In this case, your partner is your mirror, your shadow part of the soul. As a rule, this means that passive aggression is hidden in you, and you do not allow it to go out and do not even recognize it. So, if an aggressive partner appears in your life, pay attention to your own aggression and work through this resource.

If none of the above points help you, pause the relationship. Perhaps you unknowingly got into each other too deeply.

In this case, there should be a pretty decent pause - an average month (some couples take 2-3 months or, conversely, a couple of weeks). The essence of this pause - if possible, do not communicate. If you have common children, limit your circle of contacts - only household questions ("Yes, take it", "Bring it", "Yes, you need to buy this", etc.). Ideally, you should not communicate, then the intensity of unconscious destructive affect and drive in relation to each other will decrease slightly, and you will be able to look at your partner with real eyes.

Drive and effects are what are included in our consciousness when we see in a partner the parts of ourselves that we deny and our parents.

If you want the emotional intensity to fall asleep, rudeness and anger do not rage in your relationship, disperse, distance yourself from each other. This step will be painful and difficult, but it will bring the expected result - after a while you can openly look at your partner again.

Why the choice of loneliness will not bring you happiness

Loneliness is a choice and, as a rule, we unconsciously make the decision that we will be comfortable in loneliness. Can a person who has chosen such a lifestyle ("Everything. I will be alone forever!") Be happy?

Why does not choosing loneliness bring you happiness?

All lonely people (it doesn't matter - you have chosen loneliness as a lifestyle or lonely for some reason) necessarily face the opposition of modern society, especially the older generation ("Why are you single / single? It's time to find your soulmate! Or maybe are you not all right? ").

As a result of such a critical assessment of your life, each time you will feel a sense of shame and guilt, which over time will develop into open aggression ("Do not touch me! This is my life, my choice, so I live like that!"). And every time you come across this, you will feel bad. Sometimes you just need to look at your surroundings (everyone has couples, but you don't!), And there is longing, sadness and deep sadness.

If you consciously choose loneliness as a lifestyle, put up with these feelings, they will be your eternal companions. Sometimes you will feel bad.

Inside our consciousness there are objects internalized from childhood - mom, dad, grandmother, grandfather (all those people who brought us up and put something into our consciousness). Accordingly, these internal objects interact in our consciousness. Why are we getting into a relationship? To unload outwardly the experienced feelings. It is much more difficult to fight with yourself than with the person to whom we transferred the projection. In addition, to cope with all the emotions in your life on your own is quite difficult and almost impossible! A person needs to share with someone his thoughts, feelings, philosophical thoughts and life as a whole. Each of us needs someone to partially see our life, then there is no feeling of complete isolation (I am alone in the whole world!). There should be people nearby, and if they are not there, you will "bite" yourself from the inside more and more.

The consequences can be quite sad - obsessive-compulsive disorder, depressive, depressive-manic and even suicidal thoughts. Your personality will stop developing. We develop only next to other people. They are for us a mirror, our own reflection with flaws. Looking at the other, we can understand what needs to be changed in ourselves and what to accept.

If a person encounters someone in contact, and it is unpleasant for him to hear someone else's opinion about himself ("You are selfish!"), It is worth considering - is this a minus for you or a trait that needs to be accepted.

Analyze your personality, weaknesses and character traits in general - What can be improved and corrected? Why didn't you notice the feelings of another person? Or noticed, but your feelings at that moment were an order of magnitude more important?
You will not be able to work through and survive the crises of your life associated with the early period of childhood (from one year to seven years), when the foundations of the psyche were just laid. We all had some kind of crisis during this period. What does this mean?

If a person has any difficulties in his relationship, this is an opportunity to figure out in which place of his development a crisis occurred that has not been experienced. Thus, next to a real partner, he will be able to survive all those feelings that could not be experienced in childhood. However, since any psyche strives for development, a place where the crisis has not been overcome creates a kind of "traffic jam" - relatively speaking, our psyche remains to "live" at that moment in time (although we grew up, we remained small inside).

That is why a person will always feel unsatisfied, infantile, with low self-esteem. He will feel that he does not receive what he wants from the world, although he deserves much.

So, if you choose loneliness, you cannot overcome all these crises, and your psyche will "freeze" in one place. You will always feel unsatisfied in the merger area. Each of us has a need for individuation on the one hand and fusion on the other (to belong to society and to some person). Quite often, as an option to replace this merger, people choose a job or a goal. However, in the end you will want an emotional fusion with another person.

Another common reason for choosing loneliness is the fear of merging. People do not know how to enjoy this moment, and then distance themselves, so they decide to remain alone, so as not to suffer.

Does the partner compete with you?

Competition is a special kind of relationship based on the struggle for some important resource that is valuable for both members of the couple. It can be power, prestige, authority, recognition, love, financial success, etc. In a pair, partners often compete for love.

For example, today I'm small, carry me in your arms, feel sorry and comfort, and tomorrow you. If in a pair each partner wants to be circled all the time, fierce competition begins, some unpleasant feelings arise, a struggle, the level of dissatisfaction with the relations of both partners increases. Competition for success and authority is characterized by a situation where one of the partners rises sharply, for example, along the career ladder, and the second begins to languish next to him, feeling like a jerk.

In this case, there may be two options: - the one who is worse in this area immerses himself in insignificance - he is ashamed to be next to a successful partner; - the one who has achieved a certain success begins to boast of his success ("Look how everything works out for me! Here is my next success, but here I also earned (a) money without making any special effort!"). Here there is a narcissistic split between grandeur and insignificance (one of the partners assumes, relatively speaking, one pole (zone of grandeur), and the second - the other (zone of insignificance)).

Each of us, watching someone who does everything wonderful, seeks to compare ourselves with this person ("Someone did it, but I don't. So, I'm bad!"). The roots of narcissistic issues in a couple go back to childhood.

The first signs of a competitive spirit are manifested in children aged 5-6 years (sometimes even earlier!), It all depends on the level of development. The girl begins to compete with her mother for her father, or the boy begins to compete with her father for her mother. Sometimes there may be other situations - the daughter competes with her dad for her mother's attention and love (this situation mainly happens if the mother has a different man (not father)). If the family had a destructive dad (drank, rowdy, made scandals late at night, raised a hand to mom or the child himself), the girl will want her mother to divorce her dad or stepfather.

Thus, she pushes the man to the background. Having matured, she loses such a scenario in her own family - she chooses a partner who, by some criteria, is "lower than her" (externally, by status, financial income, etc.) in order to assert herself against his background, as she was unable to deal with her mother.

The boy has a slightly different situation. If there was a stepfather, and the child had to fight with him for Mom's attention, there may be two options - the relationship with the mother deteriorated, or apparently they still exist, but subconsciously the boy feels that he must always fight for the mother and her emotional response.

The essence of the problem is that a destructive coalition of unequal people is formed in the family (neither horizontally, nor vertically).

An ideal option for harmonious family relationships is a strong coalition between mom and dad, only in this case the child will have a more or less healthy understanding of what to compete for. If none of the parents provokes a spirit of rivalry in the child ("Here, fight for me!"), his desire to compete in a pair will not be included. If a similar situation occurs in the family, this suggests that neither the man nor the woman found their place in this pair (perhaps everything would have been different with another partner).

For example, in a family, mom always earned more than dad, respectively, all relatives always treated him scornfully. It is logical that the girl will have the same behavior pattern - there is nothing wrong with the fact that she earns a lot, and her career success is higher than that of her partner.

If a man had the opposite story, and dad in his family has always been an authority, earned a lot, and his mother was at home, for him such behavior of the girl will be illogical and strange. As a result, the couple will have a lot of problems: a woman will not understand why "circle" around a partner, and a man will not be able to reconcile with her irrepressible desire to work constantly.

Maybe there is such an option that the boy was against an authoritarian attitude on the part of the pope, he wanted partnerships between parents (equal earnings), or he calmly put up with parental inequality in material terms.

It's quite interesting how the quarrels in the rival pair occur. Often, one of the partners first silently accepts the success of the other, listening to the "entertaining" story of how he "put in place" some of his subordinates. However, at heart, such behavior hurts him, but the person simply does not know how to say this. After some time (a month or two), when the "successful partner" did something wrong, even at home, aggression starts at the second one ("You're such a cool boss! Now figure it out yourself and let your subordinates support you! Why are you addressing to me?").

This reaction indicates that competition has engaged. When it comes to competition, you can talk a lot about envy. Why?

To some extent, a person has low self-esteem, he believes that it's bad to be near you because of some kind of personal flaw. And if he does not have enough definite resources, power, money, authority, etc., then he is bad! This experience is so deep and painful that it is often experienced as guilt ("I should have achieved the same result!"), But more often it simply does not live, but is put somewhere in the distant box of my soul and "throw" trash from above (this feeling cannot be felt, because it hurts so much!). At the same time, a person experiences shame and sorrowful painful experiences about his personality ("I am a short-lived woman!", "I am a short-lived man!"). As a result, the unconscious provocation of your partner begins: "Are you a man at all ?!", "You don't know how to be a woman!".

Such statements are somewhat absurd - how can a person who has never been in the body of a man / woman know how it is? Behind all this often lies low self-esteem, inability to be proud of oneself, to appropriate one's own successes and skills.

Stop comparing yourself with other people, and compare only with yourself ("I have achieved a lot - and I did it, and it! If I didn't succeed, I will definitely work on this moment and will do it better next time") . We all have a different start, and this should be remembered when you start to think about whether you are worse or better than other people. These are useless and futile comparisons, because initially we are all at different levels - we were born in different families, we have different characters, genes, neural connections in the head, command patterns, etc.

What should I do if rivalries begin to appear in relationships?

Be aware of your reactions, especially if you are on the "worse" side.

Why do you consider yourself worse?

Why get involved in the competition?

Why are you jealous?

Why are you reacting aggressively?

What is going on inside you?

What do you feel when your partner begins to boast of his success?

And what happens to you when he just says something and wants to get your support or hear the joy (but you cannot be sincerely happy)?

What is the cause of your pain in this situation?

Admit your pain - "Yes, I want it too!" Why am I failing? "

If something doesn't work out for you, think about what exactly you can do.

Why isn't everything so good in your life?

Why can't you accept this fact?

Why can't you become a successful person?

A fairly common situation is when a woman puts all her energy into a man (takes care of him, cooks, tries to create home comfort, reflects on some kind of entertainment, etc.), trying to create only positive emotions around him to go towards his goal. When the partner achieves something in life, the woman begins to "destroy" all her achievements ("What am I supposed to do now? I'm completely insignificant! He achieved everything, but I did nothing!"). Know how to recognize your success in this place, your work that you have invested in the success of a partner. The ability to recognize your achievements in life (after all, you did not lie all the time on the sofa, silently looking at the ceiling!) Is a very good skill.

Remember, relationships are always collaboration. You are always together, you are in the same harness. If something happened to your partner, it means that you did it too!

And vice versa - it turned out for you, it turned out for him. In a pair, partners do everything together. Here I want to give an example from personal practice. Relatively recently, at a psychotherapy session, the girl told a story about how long and painfully she looked for work, she had to stay at home for some time, but then luck still smiled at her and offered a good position in a large company. So, the girl had long doubted whether to go or not. At the session, she said in a low voice: "Yes, my man told me - come on, go!" But I doubted so much ... ". The contribution of the young man to the solution of this issue was actually enormous, but imperceptible.

Remember, not a single person has achieved great success, recognition, love, etc. Help can be pointy or superficial, but it is worth recognizing that it still exists. If a couple of one of the partners talks about the fact that he did something, it is a joint success. Perhaps, against this background, you will begin to perceive yourself easier, because you complement each other, and not compete.

Talk with a partner. Honesty and sincerity bond relationships. If you feel an injection inside your mind ("And now what?"), Be sure to try to communicate without aggression with your loved one ("You know, you have achieved such success, and I feel like a loser next to you. You stopped noticing me, not paying attention , at home you are talking only about work ... Anyway - you are only interested in money! "). In relationships, it is important to compliment each other (this applies to both the man and the woman).

Quite often, having risen to the peak of success, one of the partners ceases to notice the other, does not give him feedback ("You are also great!", "I am so pleased to return home clean and comfortable", "I am pleased to talk with you", "This so wonderful that we can spend time together and relax, forgetting everything. Thank you for organizing all this! "). It is very important to notice what the partner is doing for you.

If you are successful, do not forget about your loved one - support him, remember all the situations in which he helped you achieve success. If you are the one who "lags behind" and feels like a jerk, directly tell your partner: "I have too little of you. I understand that dizzying success inspires you, but I would like that too. However, I do not have this, and even you are moving away. Hear my pain! "

Be vulnerable and frank with a partner in this place, do not be afraid to honestly admit your feelings. Talking about this is unpleasant, but after saying nothing, you will suffer from the fact that the partner does not notice you in his successes. Be sure to indicate the actions by which he hurt you. Learn to talk, choose the right form of communication.

It is important not only to express everything that has boiled up in the soul, the partner should hear you so as not to hurt in return.

The partner is often offended

The partner is often offended by you (it doesn't matter who it is - man or woman - the psyche has no gender in its own sense). In what situations can this happen?

If you are expressing your opinion, talk about feelings or experiences. Partner response: "You offended me, wounded me! You always criticize me and condemn me for every action! " As a result, he withdraws into himself, harboring resentment in his soul.

In fact, this is not a rejection, but a minor unpleasant situation, "bloated" by one of the partners, which cannot deeply hurt. In fact, this is a way to break contact with a person, as well as a defensive reaction.

It is worth recalling that resentment is a childish way of manipulating parents ("I'm offended, buy me a kinder, a toy ... Anyway, entertain me!").

If you look from the perspective of an adult, no one is obliged to entertain you, he's offended - deal with your insult. So, resentment is anger directed inward. One of the partners caught something inside the other, touched a painful wound, and that is why he responds so passively-aggressively. How to act in such a situation? First of all, look at yourself from the side, listen to your words, think, maybe you really are doing something undesirable for the partner, broadcasting condemnation or criticism in his direction (this often happens).

It is possible that a person close to you really has a wound in the soul or psyche, however, if you are engaged in yourself, work out exclusively your bugs that affect relationships. As a rule, people do not just meet, so there is definitely something within you. How can we broadcast?

The answer to this question is better with an example from personal practice. Recently, a client in a session said that she and her husband decided to discuss the topic of awareness. The husband said that he had once tried a narcotic substance and, according to him, it was awareness - you feel and worry everything to the smallest detail, you perceive the situation from a completely different perspective.

The woman's opinion was fundamentally different - such a state can be "caught" using higher-level techniques, for example, psychotherapy, which gives a high degree of awareness. The client has been in therapy for a long time, she knows various techniques and is comprehensively suited to solving such a problem. Accordingly, she is trying, relatively speaking, to impose on her husband a judgment: "Oh! This is such a buzz, I now probably understood the essence of this venture! " In response, she receives aggression ("You are now condemning me and shaming me!"), And although she denies that she tried to shame her husband, she admits at the psychotherapy session that she has some condemnation for people taking drugs.

So, the partner heard and felt the truth - it doesn't matter that these words were not spoken out loud, they were broadcast. Look deep into your consciousness, perhaps you really condemn the partner's behavior or criticize him for some act. In this case, he simply reads everything that is deep in your unconscious, even if you cannot fully understand it. Having dealt with yourself, you will already say these words in a different tone.

There is another interesting technique. When you voice your thoughts out loud about a heated discussion, your life together, etc. ("I condemn this method of awareness a bit, I have come across such personalities. I do not condemn you - this situation happened a long time ago, now everything is normal, you're completely different you relate to all this, and in general you have a different life "), you practically have no double messages to your partner, and he has an oppressive feeling of making claims.

This is quite an important point, so you should definitely learn to understand yourself in this situation, understand what is deep in your consciousness, and master the technique of expressing your thoughts. Another interesting case is insults in the form of "You don't hear me!", "You criticize and condemn me!" What is often the response of a partner? Yes, he does not hear me! After all, I did not mean anything like that, etc. Let me give you an example of another situation from therapy. At the session, one of the clients said: "Yes, he can't hear me at all! He says that I don't hear it, but it's not so! " To my question, "So do you hear your partner?", The woman was embarrassed and answered: "In what sense?" As it turned out, the client could not even figure out what sense the partner put into his words when he said that they did not hear him.

In fact, people really do not hear each other. The famous Argentine psychotherapist Jorge Bucay has a curious book "I want to tell you about ...", in which he interprets his unusual view of psychology, telling the reader all kinds of fables, tales and parables.

One of these parables accurately describes the situation when the couple "do not hear each other." A married couple visits a therapist. The husband calls the therapist and says: "Doctor, she's tired of me so much - she never hears how much you don't say!" Let's have a session earlier. " The therapist is trying to convince the client that he cannot take the couple at another time, and wants to understand the situation: "Tell us how you can't hear?" - Well, he doesn't hear, that's all! - Alright, call your wife. - Lena! Go here! "Where are you?" "I'm on the second floor, and she's on the first, in the kitchen." "Good, call her." - Lena! You see, he does not hear! - Go down the stairs one flight and call again. - Lena! Well, she does not hear! Doesn't even answer! - Go into the kitchen and call. - Lena! Well, what do you not answer? - Well? What? What? I've been answering you three times already, but you don't hear me! As a rule, such a story is hidden behind everything.

We are really arranged in a relationship in such a way that we want to be heard, but we don't want to hear another person. Why?

It is necessary to understand the needs of the partner, to understand the meaning of the words that he says, because they do not always convey the whole depth of a person's desire. This is a rather complicated emotional work, so it's easier to blame ("You don't hear me!").

There is another side to the coin - maybe you don't hear yourself, don't understand what needs you are trying to tell your partner. What to do?

Objectively evaluate your behavior. As a rule, the situation is "paired" - we find each other according to the degree of our injury. If one partner has an injury in this place, the second one will also find a wound in the area of shame, guilt or responsibility (depending on what it is about). For example, you blame your partner all the time, but in reality you yourself do not know how to take responsibility for your feelings, feelings, sufferings, life, etc.

Try to admit to yourself that it is, if you really want to improve relations and work out your bugs. Look deep into your consciousness in situations where you swear, and the partner is offended.

The technique works perfectly when a person comes with a certain acceptance (in the zone of his difficulties, features or injuries) from the category of humility - "Listen, I figured out myself, maybe you're right, but still there is your share of guilt ... Let's discuss my and your guilt. " This position ("50/50") allows you to inform your partner that you are also working on yourself, and this is also difficult for you. Otherwise -

with presentations and demands - no one will ever hear you. It is then that it will be easier for the partner to admit that it is difficult for him, and he also wants to work on himself. Cases when the couple often swear and at the same time do not want to "get out" of the scandals are quite rare. Basically, people want to work on themselves, but they don't understand exactly how to do it, it's hard for them to overcome the resistance associated with the fact that the partner is crushing ("Only you change, but I won't!").

Using the "humility" technique, you make it easier for your partner to change. And most importantly, do not get involved with your partner's insults by mom or dad. This is a way of manipulating parents, and you do not need to become that very parent who can be manipulated. However, don't leave your partner alone with his feelings ("I'm offended - it's my fault, these are your problems, so sort it out! And then come!"). Such tactics will provoke even greater resentment and self-closure.
I recommend saying something from the category "I'm sorry that you are so worried and perceive the situation this way ...".

This phrase will show the partner that you are emotionally involved in the situation, you do not care, but here it may sound a little different for the partner ("Well, you are so pathetic because you perceive all this!"). In some situations, it is worth lowering the degree in a relationship even further ("I'm sorry that this happens ... I'm sorry that we cannot hear each other ..."). When there is a bunch of "we", and not separately "you or me", it says that the problem is common for both partners. "We" are very united, especially in situations of quarrels and misunderstandings ("I am sorry that there is criticism and condemnation for you, but I'm definitely not trying to hurt you. Try to hear and understand inside me where this wound was formed").

If you practice psychology and listen a lot, try to convey your thought to the awareness of your partner: "Perhaps in childhood your mother told you something unpleasant, and I just got here, but believe me - not from evil! I'll definitely try to say less on this subject in a different tone, I'll work on myself, but promise me that you, in turn, will perceive the situation as an adult as a whole. "

Give your partner time to deal with this, but don't become his mother
("Let me console you, stroke ... What else can I do? Maybe buy some
candy?"). A person needs time to go through all the feelings, and at the
same time try to be near him, but do not do anything for him. When you
are nearby, you make it clear that you have not rejected and continue to
love, even if your partner is "terrible". The internal state of a person is
not important, convince him that you want to be an adult with him so
that he does not get into some kind of childhood injury. Each of us can
fall, no one is safe from this, but ideally, the partner should be close by.

So, if we are talking about a "resentful partner", this is some kind of
mutual difficulty, causing impotence, it is really difficult to get in touch
with such people.

Try to look at the situation as a new stage in the relationship. This is a
crisis of your relationship, more provoked by a partner.

As a rule, after such a crisis, when you survive all these feelings and
analyze the situation in general (how to react - what to say and what
not?), A kind of "code of rules" will be formed in the pair, and the
partners will feel comfortable in the relationship.

They don't hear me ...

All the problems and difficulties that arise in relations with a partner
should always be said out loud. However, many of you are faced with a
situation where this approach does not work - the partner simply does
not hear you, and because of this, unfortunate impotence arises. What to
do with it? And why is this happening?

Definitely do not call your partner a daffodil and disperse! Nowadays,
the scale of narcissism reaches such a colossal level that the situation
often turns into absurd and ridiculous.

In fact, the problem of "deafness of a partner in a relationship" may lie in different aspects, and not the fact that a person can be a daffodil (this happens only in 50% of cases). So, you explain something to the partner, but he does not understand.

Before putting a label on a person, making a diagnosis and breaking up relationships, let's understand all aspects of the problem. The most important criteria in the context of this question: Quite often, partners make claims and demands to each other instead of asking.

Using professional experience as an example, recently there was a couple in which partners made claims against each other during almost the entire consultation ("You didn't say that!", "I had to throw the combine! - No! I need it!", "Where are we we'll put this ?! "," Why don't you want to put it there? ", etc.). Such an exchange of claims and making claims takes a lot of time. When the partners were asked to highlight the basic need, it turned out that the man wanted to have his own space, "own corner", where he could be the master (throwing away, changing things, etc.), and the woman so that he would not touch her personal things.

First of all, we find out our deep-seated need for all claims and requirements (perhaps the essence of the problem is not a cup and a spoon, but a violation of your boundaries - you want to be respected as a person, you want to have your own space, not to constantly follow the requirements and desires partner). Then try to formulate your claim in the form of a request: "You know, I am now quite sensitive to the fact that I do not have my own place, my borders ... Let me do it the way I want, the way I feel comfortable. I want to be the mistress (master) of my words. "

Negotiate, ask and negotiate! Often in married couples people get hung up on their grievances, accumulated discontent, so they begin to unload everything to the partner at once in the form of demands.

Try to reduce the degree of aggression towards a loved one. Choose the right form of communication with your partner.

In general, this is a separate art, which should be given attention. What tone or voice we say to our partner and at what moment means a lot to him. Often we ask or say something in the same tone and words, respectively, the person doesn't get the gist of the conversation ("I'm" pecking "the same thing to him, but he can't hear me!").

Change the submission form! There is an excellent book by Joseph Zinker "In search of a good form: gestalt therapy with couples and families", in which the famous American psychotherapist "red thread" conveys to the reader the main idea of the psychology of relationships - learn to talk with a person, constantly practice this skill, try to talk about your pain, needs, requests and requests in various ways and options (even swap words!). Quite often, we try to "hammer" a thought into a person's head in the same way, but this approach simply does not suit him.

Look at yourself, analyze the form that you use. Here I want to give an example from personal experience. At about 3-4 years of gestalt education, my loved one experienced a multiple crisis (difficulties at work, family problems, etc.). I really wanted to support him, looked for various ways, tried to give advice, but I felt that all this does not help. In the end, everything turned out to be brilliantly simple - it was enough to ask the partner how to help him! The answer was ingenuous and open: "Listen, just say that everything will be fine!" Surprisingly, Gestalt teaches that the phrase "Everything will be fine!" it means absolutely nothing and is perceived by a person as "Leave me shut up, and everything will work out for you!". So, choose the form of communication and ask directly from the person how to explain to him how to help, etc. ("I would like to have this, please explain how you can convey this idea? Why are you resisting? Do you not understand my need, or what's the matter?").

Another option is to ask people close to you (from the outside) why the partner may resist and not be included in your need, tell them what exactly you are saying. As a rule, if a person listens carefully to you, it means that he is emotionally involved in this issue. In this case, you can try to use the same phrases that you use in a conversation with your partner (the main thing is to choose the right person so that the "quarrel out of the hut" is not taken out, otherwise the attitude to the family and the partner will change in the pair), and let the trusted person from the outside say how it sounds. It is beneficial for you that the partner does not understand you. Why? There may be two reasons.

First - for you the position of the offended is more familiar; the second - perhaps you are accustomed to being frustrated (in this case, it is worthwhile to carefully analyze your childhood, attachment objects, in particular the mother figure - this can be any person who was directly involved in your upbringing, had a special influence on the psyche, etc.) Most likely, you did not take something from the mother's figure, therefore, you are trying to realize this need through your partner and, as a result, make him guilty, obligated, demand something (however, in fact, the person owes you nothing). in the long run, none of the partners owes anything else. You can give something to each other (love, support, support, care, attention), but you are not obliged. That is why often a partner can look like a daffodil when you do something to see him as a rejection. This behavior is played out on purpose, but unconsciously, this is the scenario in which you are accustomed to act - deliberately talking with a partner so that he rejects you, because then it's more usual to sit and suffer ("I'm so unhappy, they reject me, they don't like me, they offend me!" .

Further, the situation is repeated one to one, as with your early object of attachment, with the mother figure. If your mother seemed to you rejecting, cold and inattentive, you will play this story in a relationship (marriage or close relationships - it does not matter). A close relationship suggests your craving for a person ("Well, please give me something that mom or dad did not give!").

Regardless of whether you are a man or a woman, each of us forms basic aspirations with our mother regarding attachment and emotional contact. If something was not enough for us in childhood, it was insulting, painful, very difficult, we transfer all this to adult relationships and, accordingly, we go and suffer - "Nobody understands me!" No matter how many partners you change, each next one will also not understand you.

Surprisingly, initially there is understanding in the relationship, the partners adjust to each other, because there is no such mask of projection (it appears only after a year, two or three). An useful recommendation regarding the selection of "necessary" words is to grow up and exit a child's position that you automatically fall into, feeling like a child next to your mother who did not satisfy your needs. You are an adult, so try to raise yourself and solve the problem in an adult way ("How else can I ask? How else can I say? How can I ask?").

It is to ask, not to demand — the child demands, the adult asks, because he understands that no one owes him anything (if he wants to, he will do it; if he doesn't want to, he will not).

The partner blames you all the time

To begin with, recognize the fact that there is something inside you that forces the other person to relieve himself of responsibility and shift the blame on you. Accordingly, you somehow translate this into contact. Your task is to figure out why others are accusing you of something that you did not do. You really take the blame (even if you are not to blame!). What to do in such a situation?

It is very important that you constantly ask yourself: "Am I guilty of what happened now?". For example, a couple went to the store to shop, but when they put the bags in the car, it turned out that the car had broken. The man's reaction: "It's all because of you, why couldn't you go tomorrow? It was necessary to buy all this today ?! " How is the breakdown related to shopping? In fact, the partner was just upset, he needed to blame someone for the problem. With his accusations, a man expresses frustration, discontent and frustration - in another way he does not know how. What should you do?

Listen calmly to the accusations and say inside yourself that your guilt is not there now ("It's not my fault that the car broke down!"). Next - act on the situation.

Immediately besiege your partner ("This is not because of me!") Or wait a few days until the passions cool, and remind of the unpleasant situation by choosing the right form of communication and tone so as not to hurt a person ("Do you really think that the car broken because of me? ").

Your task is not to take revenge on your partner by returning the pain you have experienced, but to convey to his consciousness all the illogicality and futility of such accusations. If such a task is posed, there will be no problems. If you are offended, angry (how about it - they scolded or blamed the princess (prince)!), The problem will arise unequivocally.

Extinguish resentment, anger, and injustice within yourself.

Understand that the words were not addressed to you - it is the partner's habit to respond to frustration and frustration. You are responsible for the feelings of another person. This means that you tend to assume this responsibility, you do not separate yourself and the other.

Perhaps here we can still talk about codependent relationships when you live not for yourself, but for others, fully adjusting your personality to their needs and requirements. A complex of faults from childhood. The mother figure or the family as a whole, perhaps other people who raised you, could inspire you with some responsibility for all the events taking place in the family circle.

For example: - You had infantile parents. Accordingly, you felt much more mature and responsible than them. - The mother figure blamed you all ("It happened because of you! I gave you life, but what do you give me?"), In fact, my mother had one message for her child - "you owe me." - A mother who is absent emotionally (or physically) - for example, a woman spent a lot of time at work, or was in a state of deep depression. As a result, the child takes the blame.

The main stage in the formation of the psyche falls on average between three and seven years. The baby is clearly aware - if he cries, they will take him in his arms; if shouting, feed; if shoved, they will be left alone. The whole world is reacting, which means it is doing something special for this. Only in this case, the people around him will behave as he wants.

Having matured, the child continues to think as well. At the age of 2-4, the narcissistic period begins (each child has a different way), when the whole world really revolves around a small family member ("Hello, my little one!", "What a beauty you are!", "Do you want a cookie? Or maybe maybe potatoes? "," Let's go for a walk. Why are you upset? What happened? Does something hurt? Have you fallen? ", etc.).

If the child has a guilt complex (everything in this world is due to him), he continues to think that all his actions are directly related to the response of the world. Accordingly, if the world does not react the way you want, then you did something wrong! Unhappy or emotionally cold mother — you did something wrong (you said something wrong, you did wrong (for her), your eyes were not the same, etc. In this situation, you had some kind of specific function in relation to your mother. Ask yourself, which one? How did you save your mother, console her, cheer her up, reassure her? You continue to perform this function for your partner.

This is how the guilt complex is formed when it seems that no one blamed you, but you unconsciously convinced yourself: "So, I have to do something!" In this place you have unclosed gestalt. As a result, such a person finds a partner who is always dissatisfied with life, who will constantly voice everything that "sits" in your head, confirming the most worse thoughts and fears,

in the end, he will continue to do everything that he could not do for his mother's figure (mom, dad, grandmother, grandfather - any member of the family who was more emotionally charged and turned on)! Understand this behavior - exclusively your need aw (this is not such a partner caught!).

You want to close the gestalt, show yourself on the good side ("Well done, I corrected this situation! I couldn't with my mother, but everything worked out with my partner!"). In fact, the main problem is that the situation is already impossible to correct.

Everything that is in the present tense is fictitious and covered by your projections, then you will consciously or unconsciously transmit or demand behavior that provokes the situation from childhood. What to do?

It is imperative to close that gestalt by various means and techniques. The best option is psychotherapy sessions.

Your partner is a psychopath

A psychopath is a person with antisocial personality disorder without compassion, remorse, or guilt. Such people are able to imitate normal human emotions, but do not actually experience them.

What unites absolutely all psychopaths?

Disruption of connections between the frontal and orbital parts of the brain. Both of these parts are responsible for creating emotional connections, empathy (conscious empathy with another person's current emotional state), mirror neurons, and social behavior.

Accordingly, if a violation occurs, such a person is called a psychopath. In practice, checking this condition is difficult, but there are five main signs in a person's behavior that can help you understand who is next to you. If a loved one whom you have known for many years suddenly shows psychopathic traits and behavior changes dramatically, this primarily indicates a violation of the brain's organic matter, which may be caused by trauma, the consequences of a stroke, or even a tumor.

According to the latest research by scientists, psychopathy is peculiar only to men, because Of great importance in the manifestation of this condition is the male sex hormone testosterone. However, some psychopathic traits are also characteristic of women. So, the main signs of psychopaths:

1. Lack of empathy, regret in their actions. In general, without these feelings it is very difficult to build any relationship with a partner. The manifestation of the sign is characteristic of people who do not have mirror neurons. How can one check in practice whether a partner has empathy? It is enough to pay attention to his reaction when, for example, you hit, cut your finger, tripped or fell. However, remember that at the very beginning of the relationship, the psychopath will play the role of a sensual person, will regret and sympathize (until he deserves the desired trust - after that he will be able to do whatever he wants).

2. Emotional swing. What does this mean and what does it look like in a relationship? First you will be extolled to the very heavens, you will be an ideal person ("You know how to do it so well!", "You masterfully drive a car!", Etc.). During communication on the part of the psychopath, sometimes a small opposition to himself can slip through - "Not that I am!", "I am so unhappy, I can't do anything in my life" (as if he is constantly trying to transfer the conversation to himself and complain) . Over time, the psychopath partner will show his duplicity and hypocrisy, there will be aggressive outbreaks in the conversation ("Well, of course, you are a fat woman, what to take from you?", "You don't know how to do everything on time! And you could have handed over this work earlier! »), A strange feeling of duality will appear in communication with him. If such feelings arise, you should listen to yourself - a person cannot first deify you, and then sharply lower you to the ground, while denying all your actions and possible suspicions ("It seemed to you that everything is in order!"), The tone is not the last role. That's how aggression breaks out in a psychopath (an impudent infant rage to the whole world that no one consoled in time) - the whole world owes him something, everyone around is bad, so he should take as much as possible everything "that is due to him".

Quite often, a male psychopath beats a woman, and then crawls to her in tears and on her knees to apologize, gives bouquets, gifts, beautifully courts her - "Just come back to me! I will correct myself and I will control myself! " Alas, the situation later repeats itself. By such behavior, psychopaths put pressure on the pity of a normal empathic person who can't get past the pain and not respond, and the latter turns on the narcissistic complex ("You need me, so I'll stay! You won't be able to live without me, especially now! ").

From the side of the couple it may seem completely normal, but for relatives and the immediate environment - this is an ideal partnership. In order to understand the intricacies of such relationships, you first need to separate the partners and listen to each individually. A classic psychopath will always complain that he cannot live without a partner, but he will never admit that he is unbalanced and has constant tantrums and scandals over trifles.

3. The psychopath always provokes a partner to very strong emotions. If it's love, then it's crazy. If hatred, then crazy. If tenderness, then all-consuming and limitless. It's always cool to experience all these pleasant feelings of love, joy and emotional disruption, but it's worth remembering that only psychopaths can provoke the appearance of such a huge amount of strong emotions, and this causes a certain dependence on the partner ("Well, now I'll leave, who will bring me so much joy and happiness? "). To dispel the "magic haze" of relationships, you need to remember that joy and happiness will last literally the first six months, and then will be replaced by insults, humiliations, resentments and beatings.

The partner will provoke the response of aggression, the formation of feelings of fear, guilt and shame, then to declare: "Why are you so angry? Why scared? Why are you panicking? " Why it happens?

The psychopath has an unstoppable infant rage, respectively, his container for experiences is small, and he needs a partner as a "function of the psyche" - not being able to experience and relive the feelings that surged through him, he uses the psyche of his partner as his own.

As a result, the partner will become a container of anger, fear, fear, guilt and shame. And the worst part is that when a psychopath begins to be caught lying, citing certain facts, he accuses him in response, laughs at "speculation", evades or changes the subject, saying: "Yes, everything seemed to you!" This is all untrue! " As a result, the partner is left alone with his feelings and feels guilty, outliving her for two. It is this guilt that often keeps women in such relationships. Thus, the psychopath makes maximum use of the mechanism of projective identification - all his anger is experienced by the partner, while the psychopath also criticizes him, being dismissive ("What are you saying?", "How could you?", "You yourself are aggressive ", Etc.) and shifting onto it the whole spectrum and severity of the emotions experienced.

4. Quite often, psychopaths engage their partner in a love triangle (both explicitly and not actually) ("Look, all women admire me!"). As a result of such a statement, the partner suddenly begins to be very jealous (even if he is not peculiar to jealousy), and given that the psychopath is not able to experience this feeling, the sensations intensify. The response of a person with psychopathic features of character will be very predictable - he will convince you that the problem is not in him, but in your strong reaction.

Psychopaths are selfish, require too much attention to themselves - everything should revolve only around them. For example, if a man came home from work, you should quit everything and be near - to cook, clean, put a plate of food exactly where he wants it, cut everything in the order he wants.

5. Next to a psychopathic person, your self-esteem falls "below the baseboard" - you don't recognize yourself, you feel a joyless existence and a complete lack of energy (you go to work like a robot, return home or just live day after day for life). Where is the inner drive and energy, strength and joy, pleasure, love and deification? Forgotten a long time ago. From the beginning of the relationship, the whole spectrum of emotions is lived for a period of three to six months, and then humiliation begins, psychopathy manifests itself, and the partner fully uses you to act out his feelings. Often in such a relationship a person comes to his senses only after a year ("Something is wrong with me!").

This is the first sign that the relationship is toxic to you (even if the partner is not a psychopath, you lose your identity next to him, it may be worthwhile to carefully analyze the current situation and eventually put an end to the relationship). There may be a reverse situation - you, in principle, feel bad in any relationship. That is why, before making a radical decision, it is worth consulting with a psychologist. Who can get into a relationship with a psychopath?

Absolutely each of us, but one will leave the relationship, and the other will begin to prove his innocence and rightness. Often, the "victims" of a psychopath are people with low self-esteem and lack of self-confidence, that is, individuals with not very strong identities (there is no support within their consciousness - goals, hierarchy of values, understanding of life in general (here I am to blame, and you are responsible for this you)).

The psychopath always gets injured and leads the partner as a puppet, using his emotional shock. How to check if your partner is a psychopath?

At the initial stages of the relationship, you need to pretend that you completely trust this person, are madly in love and do not notice anything, but you should carefully look at the person's behavior and soberly evaluate all his actions (relaxing, the psychopath will always show his true face).

Why a man loses interest in a woman

During a certain period of relations (including marriage), many women begin to wonder why a man lost interest in them.
The first and most important reason is alas, but time is inexorable.

The reality is that absolutely all relations in the first 1-1.5 years are built on a candy-bouquet period, when a pair of partners do not notice each other's shortcomings or any negative qualities or do not focus on this.

However, over time, you begin to notice everything, get annoyed, express accumulated negative thoughts to your partner.

It is important to understand that men are no exception here - their feelings are also weakening, and the woman, who was previously a "new exciting book", became understandable and predictable in her actions. Many aspects of partner behavior are quite clear, albeit superficially (in fact, it is no longer necessary for a man).

There is another option - often people just do not know how to look deeply at many things, events and in general around. Yes, we know some superficial story about each other, but we never thought about the feelings experienced by a loved one, especially what worries him now, what deep feelings he experiences and why.

Paradoxically, it is this factor that is the "secret" of a rather happy marriage - when people agree to a similar average interest in each other, relatively speaking - to an average level of arousal. In addition, in this case, much less negative moments are experienced.

The next reason is your own fault, which is completely unrelated to clothing, hair or communication with a partner. The true reason is that you yourself have lost interest in yourself. Any woman as long as she is interested in herself is interesting to those around her. And at that moment when she ceases to be interested in herself, those around her also "go out" in relation to her. Yes, and she loses the ability to notice the sparkle in the eyes of other people who look at her (and her husband is no exception!). A similar problem can also manifest itself in a codependent relationship, when a woman thinks too much about her spouse ("How can you please? Have I cooked delicious borscht? Did you dress beautifully? Did I do it well, could it have been different?") .

In fact, she loses her identity next to her partner and becomes uninteresting to him. If the situation is familiar to you, first of all, return your interest in life and in yourself (remember what you aspired to, what you dreamed about (or dreamed earlier). At least, you will be interested in living. The last reason is that a man, in principle, is not capable of long keep an interest in something or someone else. And you are not an

exception - this is the male psyche. He superficially figured out
something - quit, it's not interesting.

Such people in the business are called startups and are recommended to
work in tandem with those who can do the same job for a long time,
tediously and monotonously after the business has started to develop
stably.In relationships, this manifests itself rather unpleasantly - the
woman understands that the partner did not fully recognize her soul and
emotions, does not understand her reaction, and the man on the
contrary, I believe that everyone already knew, and he is not interested
to understand more.

Why do good girls fall for bad boys

Cases when good people fall in love with the "bad" quite often. Why is
this happening?

Explanation can be found in the theory of Ronald Fairbairn (the famous
British psychoanalyst, one of the founders of the theory of object
relations). What is libido? How is it formed?

Libido is an unconscious sexual desire or sexual instinct, the foundation
is laid in early childhood (in fact, in infancy - mainly before the age of
one). In infancy, each person perceives the maternal figure (or other
people who care about him) as an object. In addition, the child "splits"
the mother into "good" and "bad" (psychoanalysts call it a little
differently - "good" and "bad" breasts). What does this mean?

A good mother is one who feeds well and on time, satisfies all the needs
of the baby at the first call. Bad, respectively, does the opposite. In fact, it
implies emotional contact with the child and how fully the baby is
satisfied. However, one "eat" is not enough. In addition, the mother
should be comforted, picked up, looked into her eyes, stroked and so on.

Such moments eventually add up in two boxes - one with good messages from mom, the second with bad ones. With age, the image of the mother is integrated, a person begins to perceive it holistically. There is a reverse situation - one of the options is chosen (either the mother is exceptionally perfect, or exceptionally good). In this case, we can say that the integration has not occurred. In adulthood, good and bad boxes do not disappear anywhere. All that has been identified in the "good breast" area, a person is trying to find in his partner (relatively speaking, this is the tip of the iceberg).

Thus, all the good things that were in the mother's figure and the people who took care of the child (dad, grandfather, grandmother) accumulate in a good box, then the person sees all these qualities in the chosen partner and falls in love. However, in fact, they are attracted not by positive aspects, but by the unconscious (resentment, disappointment, frustration, deprivation, which were accumulated and hidden in the "bad" chest). Why it happens?

The psyche is designed in such a way that all unmet needs from childhood do not disappear anywhere, emptiness remains in their place, and consciousness tries to fill it. In addition, there remains an incomplete gestalt, which requires replacement with another similar object (to improve not only the situation, but also itself).

Thus, consciousness works with certain goals - to find a similar object, make it treat itself differently (with great respect and acceptance), and satisfy its needs. Accordingly, the methods of satisfying these needs will not change and will remain the same as in childhood.

You can add a few more to Fairbairn's theory: We fall in love only with people who are similar to ourselves. Jungian theory - everyone has a good and a bad side. We recognize the first, and reject the second, trying to hide away. As a result, a person is looking for his shadow part in a possible partner. The search for a partner is based on the principle of "what needs to be worked out in oneself". This is a mirror image - a partner is needed in order to know himself better, he reflects all those qualities that have remained unworked. Any psychological trauma or dissatisfaction requires an exit.

That is why the existing or former partner was not chosen by consciousness by chance. This is a signal that a person rejects some part of himself, as a result, the psyche pushes him to know himself better through another. How to fix this unconscious pattern, stop being attracted to "bad" people, eliminate destructive love?

Examine yourself, your childhood, deal with psychological trauma. To realize the existence of a problem, to understand the needs that cause destructive relationships.

Change the direction of your attraction and the overall pattern of behavior. The last point is quite difficult to perform. Some people take years of therapy to do this. It all depends on the rigidity of the psyche of the personality, on average, it takes more than a year to change such deep patterns.

In order to learn how to be attracted to the "right" person, to see the good in the good, not to depend on internal aspirations and not to suffer from this, you need to work on yourself for a long time and hard.

Fear of being abandoned

In contrast to the fear of rejection, which is based on a sense of shame for experienced needs and personal characteristics, the fear of being abandoned is much deeper, reminiscent of panic horror from a state of oblivion, non-existence. How to understand if a person has this fear? What are the causes of its occurrence? How to deal with it?

In general, the origins of this condition should be sought in early childhood, under the age of one year. For example, a small child abandoned by parents at grandparents (this is a basic safety hazard), a high level of mother's anxiety for the fetus during pregnancy (in this case, the child inside the womb and during the first year of life acutely perceives the mother's condition), serious injury, surgery , hospitalization after birth, any threat to life associated with a panicky feeling of fear of being abandoned or being alone.

In psychology, a condition is called a "trauma of abandonment" or a "trauma of abandonment" (James Hollis). Like any feeling, this fear has a continuum from the mild anxiety that every person has to a greater or lesser extent (for example, fear of spiders, darkness, meeting a tiger, etc.), to extreme unbearable horror (a person has various dissociative sensations - I do not exist, I leave my body and watch myself from the side), up to the traumatic state of affect. Directly, the depth of the injury will directly depend on how early the person was abandoned in childhood, who abandoned, whether there were resources to cope with the anxiety state. What adolescents may fear being abandoned?

These are people who do not have a basic trust in the world, others, even in themselves. They constantly expect a trick from the partner, they are afraid that they will turn away from them and leave, therefore they try to control the situation, including the behavior of the partner. Relations with such a person are quite complicated.

The general psychological state of an anxious personality is unstable and painful - the absence of a relationship leads to a feeling of non-existence, loss of oneself, and while in a relationship, a person constantly fears being abandoned again. In addition, over a period of time while a person was trying to cope independently with the grief of loneliness, he learned to live alone and rely only on himself. Accordingly, trusting the world and the people around you with an anxious personality will be quite difficult.

In these moments, the problem is very reminiscent of the fear of rejection. As a rule, a person independently finds situations that reproduce a trauma experienced earlier, unconsciously seeks to be abandoned, or finds an unstable person in a relationship (with a similar fear or devaluing). What should a person with such an injury do? To realize the presence of a trauma of abandonment, to accept it, regardless of the desire of the person, it is there and will not disappear anywhere, and from time to time, a person will fall under the influence of an experienced emotional shock.

Decide that he will not succumb to the fear of being abandoned. Believe in yourself (each person is interesting and worthy of love and attention in his own way); to understand that in life there is surely a person who is ready to appreciate and accept all the features of the character of his partner. To learn to track situations that indicate that a person falls into the funnel of injury, and try to stop them with an effort of will. Learning to manage your fears, to become taller, to develop self-confidence (for example, "No, they will not leave me. This situation is completely different from my childhood trauma. I am now an adult, I know that my partner loves me"). to study the moments of his unconscious behavior, aimed at ensuring that the partner turns away (this will allow a detailed analysis of the current situation). Surround yourself with people you can trust. They must become an external resource for support. Be sure to get feedback from them. Learn to open up to people, but be very attentive and carefully select interlocutors for frank conversations.

Come up with phrases that will act soothingly. To write down and use them as a mantra, for example, "I will never allow me to do this again. I will live better, because I am worthy of love and acceptance! Everything will be fine this time. " Is it possible to deal with this injury on my own? What difficulties can be?

First of all, it is quite difficult to identify the fact of the presence of such an injury (for example, no one to ask). As for the trauma received inside the mother's womb, it is doubly more complicated - the mother may not tell about her fears and worries anxieties. In addition, it will be difficult for a person who has experienced feelings of abandonment to trust themselves and others, to realize that they can really love her, to accept themselves with all the shortcomings.

If a person does not trust his own feelings, he will not be able to understand the funnel of injury and understand at what stage the traumatic experiences turn on, it will also be difficult to get rid of internal anxiety. What approaches and techniques can still help? Various body-oriented techniques, trainings, seminars.

After visiting each training session, it is recommended to consult a psychotherapist to discuss the experience gained (on average, 2-4 sessions).

Passion in relationships

Speaking of emotions, there is one simple truth that can change our view of things when it comes to tense situations:

When a person experiences a strong emotion, he ALWAYS tries to make you feel this emotion too.

So conflicts swell.

For example, something does not work out for her husband during the training camp. The dishes are flying out of my hands, the pass to the office has gone somewhere. Feeling anger, and underneath it - powerlessness, while addressing his wife, the husband will subconsciously arrange his actions and remarks in such a way that the wife will also experience powerlessness, even if before that she was in a cheerful mood.

For example, a husband can say to his wife offering help: forever you go crazy with your advice! The wife will feel unnecessary and petty, unable to help. Powerless. The irritation that accompanies powerlessness will capture her flow, and if this woman does not have a sufficiently high level of awareness, she will irritably respond to her husband's remark, inflating his powerlessness.

If you caught yourself in a cycle of inflating each other's emotions, on which side of the barricade you might be (the initiator or the defendant), note that this dynamic is happening. The more willing you are to notice this type of energy exchange and the discharge of negative emotions, the faster it will become possible to track the onset of the "transfer" of emotions and choose the next answer consciously, instead of adding fuel to the fire while playing such games.

It is important to understand that we all resort to this behavior, but not everyone is able to consciously control this behavior. The fact is that this mechanism of relieving emotional stress is formed in the psyche in early childhood: when we are sad, when we are angry, we subconsciously try to draw another person into our reality, sharing with him an unpleasant feeling that exceeds our ability to hold discomfort.

What to do when you notice that you started to get involved in the cycle of transferring emotions to each other? First, note that in a relationship you don't have to share negative emotions with your partner to help him deal with it. When you notice that a loved one is out of sorts, direct your efforts to creating a space where he can express his emotion in safety and without consequences.

Most of us grew up in families, where it was dangerous to express our emotions in their fullness and sincerity. In a family where emotions are divided into "right" and "wrong", there is no room for self-expression, and a person has to look for roundabout ways to survive (for example, identification with the physical body and subsequent lack of integration into the physical plane of being, suppression of "wrong" emotions and fragmentation of the psyche). Creating a safe space for expressing emotions allows a person to experience an inexperienced experience. Such a space itself is healing in its essence.

Secondly, you need to learn how to maintain a good and understanding attitude towards your partner. We all sometimes feel inadequate, powerless, angry, grumpy, irritated. Such emotional states do not mean that we do not deserve love, or that we are rejected by nature. We live in a dual world built on a game of opposites. Denying a whole camp of emotions that, moreover, is not possible to control, is at least naive.

Become an expert in understanding another person. Please note that in his behavior, in his reaction to a number of certain events, there is a pattern.

Pay attention to how this person expresses himself when this and that and that happens to him. It would be foolish to expect that the next time the event recurs, a person begins to behave differently. However, it is precisely because we expect a different reaction - a more positive, conscious, or some other one that we like more - we get annoyed and become unable to interact with our loved one in the moment.

Your preservation of a high wave and unobtrusiveness in the proposal of a solution to a loved one (or rather, generally refraining from giving advice until another person expresses a desire to discuss the situation) is a prerequisite for the unpleasant emotion lived by another person to quickly lose its charge.

Thirdly, you need to give a person living an unpleasant state to feel that you are not abandoning him at that moment when this state overcomes him. The reason we are afraid of our emotions is because people who have been taking our love away from us throughout our lives have cost us to express emotions that are uncomfortable for them.

Being close to a person who is depressed, experiencing suicidal thoughts, tears and mosques, or in any other way expresses his emotional truth, which is unpleasant for us, hard and energy-intensive. At the same time, if this person is important to you, it is in your right to choose to stay next to him, not moving to his emotional state, but allowing him to express himself in its entirety. We must make it clear to our loved ones that our love for them is not based on any emotional expression. Provided that emotional expression does not prompt a person to resort to violence against you, the moment of expression of negative emotions can become the moment of release of suppressed energies, bringing to all sides of the interaction a calm and balanced state of mind.

Get out of a toxic relationship

There is a lot of literature on this subject, it would seem that people are becoming more and more informed about what NOT should be a relationship.

But, despite this, the number of clients who come to me in therapy with the topic of unhealthy relationships, the number of similar topics in the forums, is growing every month and year.
* The girl, who was beaten for several months, managed to find the strength to leave the young man, but being not with him, recalls the good moments of their relationship and believes that she still loves this man.
* A woman who has suffered from a relationship with a psychopath is tormented for months by internal dialogues and wants to explain to her offender what he was wrong about.
* The woman whom the husband makes claims every day, humiliates, believes that this is what she deserves and the best in life she will not have ...
* The girl, despite the insults of the man, returns time after time with his things to his apartment and continues to live with him further, believing in his promises to change.

All of these stories have one thing in common. All these women are in a toxic relationship or have not emotionally quit. To do this, indeed, is not easy. Studying numerous cases and helping people in a situation of toxic relationships, I have identified several reasons why it is difficult for people to get out of such relationships:

Low self-esteem, which follows from the deep beliefs that a person has heard from his close people throughout life. "But who will love you like that?", "Marry anyone, then there will be no chance with your character", "Nothing, I put up with it and you will bear it." Infected with these beliefs, people choose the path of a toxic relationship. In therapy, we analyze such beliefs, and this becomes the first step towards the formation of an adequate self-esteem and self-worth.

Belief that the partner will change and hope for a bright future with him. Moreover, a person trapped in a toxic relationship experiences compassion for a partner who confuses feelings of love. In such relations, too much importance is attached to those bright and good periods that were between the partners, and this gives hope that the person will change. A woman in such periods even wants to protect her partner as a small child, her duty in such periods is to bear resentment and endure humiliation. When the victim of such treatment meets kindness in his address, she begins to feel obligated and remains in a relationship to pay this "debt". Unfortunately, the stronger the illusion that a person occasionally shows kindness because he loves, the more painful it is to look at reality.

Therapy helps a person to look at the reality in which he finds himself and accept the fact that the person with whom he is in a relationship is not healthy, that it is impossible to change him and that these relationships destroy his life.

Adjustment for a partner on an emotional level. The more a person adapts to his partner in toxic relationships, the more he becomes attached to him. In this tweak, a steady unconscious belief appears that you need to take responsibility for the emotional state of the partner and his needs. Therapy helps not only to "give" to the partner his responsibility for his needs, emotions, but also to see what you can rely on in this situation and regain what you lost in the relationship.

Fear of being abandoned. Not having a positive experience of love and care on the part of parents, a woman in her personal relationships begins to take care of a man, to please him because of fear of being alone.

Guilt. A person begins to analyze the reasons for his actions and the actions of his partner. Such internal dialogues prevent a person from getting out of these relationships on the emotional, and sometimes on the physical level. A person is looking for answers to his questions and this can last for years ... In the treatment of such questions are the answers. By not torturing oneself with guilt, but by sharing responsibility for everyone's behavior in a relationship, a person's chances are faster to get out of these relationships and end them on an emotional level.

Poisoning humor in relationships

Mockery, humor, jokes, jokes ...

On the one hand, these are some harmless things that can bring freshness, novelty, and even pleasure and joy to a relationship.

On the other hand, all this is good when it is mutual. When this mutual game-exchange of jokes brings pleasure to both partners in a relationship and, most importantly, that they feel comfortable at the same time. But there are other situations where ridicule can be a form of psychological violence.

I will give you some examples from my practice and observations of my friends. "He constantly attacks me, asks some questions, it seems to me that I should justify myself to him. But when I start to defend myself, answer questions, defend my opinion, he translates everything as a joke, starts laughing, or just might say: "I've joked!" From such "jokes" everything inside me is tightly compressed, and I feel tension. Then we can translate the topic, but after a while everything repeats itself again. "

This woman tells that her husband's tricks, his laughter, where she is not funny, bring her discomfort. I want to run away so as not to hear what is unpleasant, so as not to make excuses, becoming a victim. It takes a lot of effort to withstand this tension, a feeling of anger, injustice appears. Anger in this situation is a marker that borders have been violated.

This is a bell to the fact that humor in these situations is not something bringing together, giving pleasure. On the contrary, it is an obstacle to a full and high-quality contact that would satisfy both partners.

Here we clearly see that from harmless communication with jokes and jokes for one, it turns into suffering and pain for another, even at the bodily level. "My husband and I have long been accustomed to communicate with each other in the language of humor, we often make fun of each other, we can tease each other.

Sometimes these are harmless phrases, but sometimes you have to hear catchwords and "harder". I am not in debt either. " Let's analyze this option. It would seem that everyone is happy with everything, this is such an unwritten rule in a relationship that "it's customary to joke with each other, and there's nothing like that." People have adapted to each other and, perhaps, get some pleasure from it. Even insults, and somewhere profanity do not go through the filter of respect in a relationship.

For some couples, this tension in the relationship brings its own special acuteness, zest, and even maintains a passion for each other. It seems that on this mutual launching of arrows at each other, sincere feelings of love and care are supported, but this is not so. All this reminds me of some sort of sado-masochistic game organized by people with a neurotic character. Neurotics feel internal insecurity, vulnerability and inferiority.

To defend themselves against their partner and the world at large, they begin to attack. Often, neurotic behavior takes the form of indirect (unconscious) and verbal aggression in order to throw off your emotional stress. Expressing your aggression in the form of anger and anger is not always socially acceptable, it harms relationships and leads to conflicts.

Humor and ridicule become a "salvation" for relieving stress, but it can also humiliate and suppress another partner. At the same time, the neurotic himself believes that he is acting correctly and appropriately (as we see in the first case: "Yes, I was joking!"), Not taking his partner's words seriously, devaluing his feelings and behaving insultingly.

Thus, partners become some kind of scapegoats, containers for relieving tension that occurs in a relationship. Behind this tension are deeper, unconscious human needs, which are not expressed directly, but find a "workaround". Relief in the form of jokes cannot pass without a trace for a relationship.

Partners lose their self-esteem, the sexual sphere suffers, mutual understanding and warmth leave relationships, they become more superficial. And more and more people are moving away from themselves, not realizing that this form of communication destroys him...

Difficulties of remarriage

Divorce. A lot of painful emotions are associated with this condition.

For some people, divorce becomes such a traumatic situation that they hesitate to enter into a new relationship. Others, in spite of their own fears, have a sincere desire to get acquainted, create a new family, raise common / non-common children.

After a divorce from one and / or both partners on the basis of distrust of the former spouse, caused by disappointment, the bar of how the new partner should be, increases. And certainly this partner should be better than the previous one.

This kind of attitude suggests that people have already been burned once, and are striving with all their might to avoid this pain in the future. Therefore, the first thing that needs to be done is to take the experience out of the divorce, to understand for itself the significance of this situation. This is much better than being resentful, angry, jealous of your former partner, suffering and blaming yourself and your partner for what happened.

 "Having suffered" in the old relationship, having experienced a painful divorce, the man / woman thinks that since they have already gone through all these difficulties, then everything should be fine, "it cannot always be bad." Here they fall into the trap of their expectations, which can be idealized, as people hope for a miracle. Or that another partner will heal them from the pain of their first marriage. But this is not so. Because people always remain people - with their needs, desires, character and habits. And the more illusions and expectations from the new partner, the more painful it is to be disappointed when the partners get to know each other better and understand that their hopes have not come true.

There may be difficulties in a new marriage that are influenced by past experience in the relationship of one or both spouses.

The first variant of the influence of this experience is an unfinished situation of relations with the former spouse and emotions associated with it that a person brings to his new relationship. For example, when the ex-husband was late at work until late, his wife thought that he was cheating on her. She transfers this experience of perception to a new relationship and any delay in her work partner "plunges" her into those unpleasant thoughts, the reactions to which are corresponding. This leads to conflict, disagreement. It is important at the beginning of the relationship to be able to negotiate with your partner, talk about yourself, about your experience, about your feelings, desires and needs. And also to monitor what feelings belong to the former spouse, and what emotions are to the present. In such situations it will be appropriate to ask oneself: "What am I worried about now, why am I worried?" This awareness will help to understand what kind of need is behind these feelings and will give a person a choice - what can be done about it.

The second variant of the influence of past experience on new relationships is related to the fact when one of the spouses dies in marriage. And it seems that in past relationships the woman felt bored, was somewhat unsatisfied with her partner, but the very fact of death "obliges" to remember only good things about him. When a new partner does something wrong, behaves in a certain way, this leads to a comparison in favor of the ex-husband. This complicates the relationship. You need to understand that the partners had their own life before the second marriage, and the husband occupied the main place in it.

This means that a person has the right to memories. There are situations when a new spouse asks to throw out all the photos, some memorabilia, dear to the heart gifts associated with past relationships. In other words, abandon the past. It's like a man says: "If these things and memories are dear to you, it means that those relations are dear to you, and not the relations with me." This is characteristic of people with low self-esteem. But at the same time, too careful, but at the same time, demonstrative attitude to the past, can also cause conflicts and jealousy.

Most often, people entering into a second marriage already have children, and this creates certain difficulties in interacting with a spouse.

When a third person enters into the relationship of mother and child, he may begin to introduce some rules without establishing a relationship with the child. The spouse should first understand what is happening in the family, and only then act.

The situation is further complicated by the fact that a woman does not always understand what she wants from a man in relation to her children. On the one hand, she does not really want to impose her children on her new spouse. On the other hand, a woman may need a man to influence her children, who are still strangers to him. Moreover, if the spouse also has children with whom he comes into a new family, the woman tries by all means to become a mother for them. But you need to understand that the implementation of the practical functions of mom or dad does not mean that for the child, the spouses have become real parents. Moreover, for children, entering into a new relationship is associated with a sense of fidelity towards another parent. This can be described as: "I will betray my dad if I treat my mother's new man well or love him." And if for a woman / man remarriage is the end of a period of loneliness, for children it is the beginning of a difficult stage where there is the pain of loss.

In the relationship between the parent and the child, there are many different habits, jokes, some rituals that may not always be clear to the new partner.

It is very important not to hush up, to show interest in their relationship, not to think about what "if I wanted to, I would tell". To this are added old friends, hobbies, for whom one should also look for a place in a new relationship. What to do in all these difficulties when the family has children?

Of paramount importance are conversations with the spouse on these topics in order to avoid quarrels in the future. It is also important for each member of the family to determine their place in the family, to give them rights, obligations, and authority. To achieve clarity in this interaction so that subsequently there is no confusion and misunderstanding.

There are situations that cannot be resolved, and therefore spouses and children should come to terms with this fact, look for common ground, seek pleasure from those things that bring joy to everyone.

The ability to accept a situation as it is depends on how everyone will feel in a new relationship.

Family scenarios in relationships

When creating a family, each of the partners brings its expectations and ideas to it, endows these relationships with their dreams and goals, draws a picture of the desired future.

In addition to these intentions and ideas, the basis of family relations is also based on a lot of unconscious beliefs about how to create a family, which we borrow from our parents and subsequently reproduce in our own relationships. These attitudes and rules, on the basis of which we strive to build relationships in the family, repeating the parental model, have a very beautiful name - "family scenarios".

Family scenarios are patterns of interaction between family members, repeated from generation to generation, due to certain events in the family history. Family scenarios include beliefs and beliefs about how to live, family myths and ideology, rules and taboos, on the basis of which family members build their interaction with other family members, as well as with the outside world.

These scenarios can relate to absolutely any aspect of family life: how many children there are ("in our family no one gives birth to more than one child"), money ("there have never been any rich people in our family - there is nothing to strive for"), professional activity (" we are a dynasty of musicians "), role positions (" women in our family devoted themselves to children and the family "), everyday life (" our house is always open for guests "), etc.

Family scenarios have much in common with family traditions and rituals, but unlike the latter, they sometimes dramatically affect a person's fate, and not just color everyday life. The reasons for the emergence of certain scenarios are usually not recognized by family members, and following them is taken for granted and sometimes even the only true course of events. But there are always reasons, just not always, even the one who became the ancestor of the family scenario realizes a causal relationship. Many cases are known when, for example, in a family from generation to generation women choose husbands to be their husbands, who left them soon after the birth of the child.

Typically, such stories are usually interpreted as "evil rock" or "the unfortunate fate of women of the genus." But from a psychological point of view, in such family stories there is nothing surprising and nothing otherworldly.

It is simply likely that three or four generations ago a woman who could not build her family relationships formed certain beliefs about men - that they are all rascals, unreliable, they can not be trusted. Such beliefs at one time helped her to cope with the reality and consequences of a failed family life. And they were also called upon to protect her from repeated such a painful experience.

It is quite natural that the same beliefs and attitudes towards men were subsequently transferred to her daughter, both consciously - through intimidation, threats, exhorting her from relationships, and unconsciously. A girl brought up by a mother with such a set of beliefs will subconsciously choose not a trustworthy man as her partner, because she does not have experience of trusting relations with a representative of the opposite sex (father), but will project her mother's fears and attitudes that have already become her internal introjects (imposed from the outside by unconscious rules that govern behavior). In the end, this can lead to the fact that again the family scenario will be reproduced - "followed in the footsteps of the mother."

Such an example is one of the most "classic" ones to illustrate the work of family scenarios. But there is also a mass of not so dramatic and not so obvious manifestations of family scenarios in a relationship. For example, the desire to leave the parental home as soon as possible in "free swimming", which succumbed to young people in each generation, or the age of marriage.

It happens that family scenarios are so firmly rooted that it becomes self-evident for the script carrier: to get married, for example, it is necessary strictly up to 30, or in no case should you get married before 35. It must be understood that the family scenario itself is not inevitable , not a sentence or diagnosis.

Each family system (and the family from the point of view of family psychologists is a system) assumes the existence of scenarios that are reproduced from generation to generation. Indeed, in essence, these scenarios are designed to protect against the dangers and uncertainties of this world (for example, the scenario of avoiding wealth subsequently dispossessed in previous generations, formed on the conviction that "money is dangerous").

But it happens that a certain scenario no longer just protects, but even hinders the creation of happy family relationships (as, for example, a scenario creates only status marriages and avoids real intimacy in a relationship, because it implies vulnerability). In this case, it is important to see and realize this recurring plot, to look at it not as the only possible option, but just as one of the many possible scenarios for the development of events. This may require personal psychotherapy, because it is sometimes difficult to move away from the usual family "plot" because of the strong emotional load of the latter. Is it necessary to eradicate all family scenarios taken from parental families that you may already find in your married life? Obviously not.

It is likely that such family repetitions will become only a pleasant, family-holding tradition (for example, having many children, which will become a distinctive family feature that brings joy to all members of the family system). But if the family scenario is contrary to the scenario of the spouse, then sometimes serious conflicts can arise and even relations can be broken, because deviation from the usual family scenario, absorbed from early childhood, can cause tension, anxiety and even fear.

For example, on the basis of family attitudes and rules, a woman wants to realize the scenario of "early motherhood" - only this option of development of events seems correct and most obvious to her immediately after the creation of the family. And her partner, on the contrary, has a clear attitude about the fact that children should appear only after the spouses are confidently standing on their feet - he seeks to realize his scenario of responsible parenthood, imitating his father. Obviously, in such a clash of antagonistic scenarios, a serious conflict is inevitable. In this case, it is very important to find the true sources of your aspirations, dig up programs and scripts that unconsciously seek to be reproduced, and find your true needs that need to be realized. And then to conduct a dialogue - both with yourself and with your partner, in order to come to a compromise that will satisfy everyone, and not just in words.

There is nothing wrong with the family scenario. The danger lies only in the fact that if a person builds his life only by reproducing parental attitudes or family scenarios, it turns out that he does not live life, but life "lives it".

It is important to realize what decisions we make in life and why, what motivates us, what needs and values we satisfy, what script we write. And if at some point you realize that you are repeating the scenario of your family system, and this causes a pleasant smile from understanding a fate somewhat similar to other members of your kind, then do not rush to change everything at all costs, just not "according to the script."

Well, if, when analyzing your life, you find that there are many sad similarities, it is better to turn to a deeper analysis of the causes of your actions and take responsibility for your life.